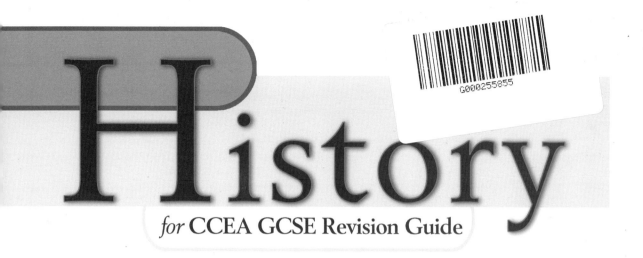

History

for CCEA GCSE Revision Guide

Finbar Madden

Hodder Murray

A MEMBER OF THE HODDER HEADLINE GROUP

The Publishers would like to thank the following for permission to reproduce copyright material:
Photo credits p. 11 Bettman/Corbis; p. 132 Bettman/Corbis
Acknowledgements CCEA GCSE History Compendium 2003–2005 © 2003–2005 with the permission of the Northern Ireland Council for the Curriculum, Examinations and Assessment
Every effort has been made to trace all copyright holders, but if any have been inadvertently overlooked the Publishers will be pleased to make the necessary arrangements at the first opportunity.

Although every effort has been made to ensure that website addresses are correct at time of going to press, Hodder Murray cannot be held responsible for the content of any website mentioned in this book. It is sometimes possible to find a relocated web page by typing in the address of the home page for a website in the URL window of your browser.

Orders: please contact Bookpoint Ltd, 130 Milton Park, Abingdon, Oxon OX14 4SB. Telephone: (44) 01235 827720. Fax: (44) 01235 400454. Lines are open 9.00–5.00, Monday to Saturday, with a 24-hour message answering service. Visit our website at www.hoddereducation.co.uk

© Finbar Madden 2007
First published in 2007 by
Hodder Murray, an imprint of Hodder Education, an Hachette Livre UK company
a member of the Hodder Headline Group
338 Euston Road
London NW1 3BH

Impression number	5	4	3	2	
Year	2010	2009	2008	2007	

Cover photo Peter Kemp/AP/PA Photos; MPI/Getty Images; AKG-images
Typeset in 10.5 on 13pt Frutiger by Phoenix Photosetting, Chatham, Kent
Printed in Malta

A catalogue record for this title is available from the British Library

ISBN: 978 0340 939 918

CONTENTS

AIMS OF THE BOOK

Welcome to *History for CCEA GCSE Revision Guide*. This book has been written to help you achieve the best mark possible in your GCSE History examination. However, before we start looking at the specifics of GCSE History in detail, let's see if you can answer the following (simple) question:

What are the two most basic things that you need to have to pass any examination?

No, it's not a trick question; if you hope to pass an exam, no matter what the subject, you need:

(a) Knowledge of the facts;
(b) The skills to enable you to put your knowledge down on the script in a manner that will gain you marks.

It's as simple – and as difficult – as that!

This book aims to make it simple by focusing on these key elements in the context of GCSE History. It helps to prepare you in two ways:

1. Firstly – and most basically – *History for CCEA GCSE Revision Guide* sets out the essential facts that you need to know to be able to answer the questions set. There's no way around it – you need to know this!
2. Secondly – and equally importantly – *History for CCEA GCSE Revision Guide* provides you with guidance on how to acquire and develop the examination skills that will enable you to achieve your potential in the examination. There's no point in knowing it if you can't put it down on paper in time!

The book is structured into the main topics in the specification. Each topic is then divided into sections that mirror the divisions outlined by CCEA in the specification for GCSE History. Each section is then divided into appropriate sub-sections designed to break up the knowledge content into easy-to-manage pieces. Each sub-section contains a summary of the key facts relevant to that part of the course as well as a number of simple revision tasks. As you read through and come to grips with the facts you should find that completing these tasks will:

1. Enable to you to understand the facts more fully;
2. Provide you with easy-to-remember revision tables and diagrams.

All the way through the text you'll find words and phrases highlighted in bold. These are examples of the kind of subject-specific terminology that you can expect to encounter in some parts of the examination and whose correct use will undoubtedly impress the examiners. You will find these words defined in the *Glossary*, but before you look up the meanings try to work them out for yourself.

There are also plenty of knowledge tests, which will give you the chance to check if you really have those key facts safe inside your head. You'll find the answers for these listed in Chapter 6.

Perhaps most importantly, there are real CCEA GCSE History past paper questions and key points from the examiners' mark schemes for these questions. The past paper questions will give you something realistic to practise on and, having done them, you will then be able to compare your answers with what the examiners are looking for.

GETTING YOUR REVISION RIGHT

This chapter focuses in particular on outlining and developing the skills that will enable you to approach the examination with confidence. You'll find information on the course structure and an overview of how the examination is organised. You'll find suggestions on how to approach revision. Most importantly, you'll find practical information on sitting the examination, including guidelines on how much time you should spend on each question and suggestions on how to deal with the specific question styles that are used by those who set the examination.

STRUCTURE OF THE COURSE

If you want a detailed breakdown of the CCEA GCSE History specification, you can download it from the CCEA website at www.ccea.org.uk.

ASSESSMENT OBJECTIVES

The assessment objectives for CCEA GCSE History are laid out in detail in the specification. Briefly, there are three assessment objectives that focus on the knowledge, skills and abilities that the examiners are attempting to assess. The assessment objectives require candidates to demonstrate their ability to:

AO1 Recall, select, organise and deploy knowledge of the specification content to communicate it through description, analysis and explanation of:

◆ the events, people, changes and issues studied
◆ the key features and characteristics of the periods, societies or situations studied.

AO2 Use historical sources critically in their context, by comprehending, analysing, evaluating and interpreting them.

AO3 Comprehend, analyse and evaluate, in relation to the historical context, how and why historical events, people, situations and changes have been interpreted and represented in different ways.

LAYOUT OF THE EXAMINATION

This is fairly straightforward. To start off, make sure that you are doing the right sections on the day of the exam – it has been known for people to get it wrong! You have a choice of questions to answer in both parts of Paper 1 and some choice with the essay in Section B of Paper 2. Before deciding which questions you are to do, glance over all the questions quickly, noting any areas where you feel particularly strong (or weak). Then, on the basis of this, make your question choice and stick with it!

Here's how the papers break down:

Paper 1

- Lasts 2 hours.
- Is worth 50 per cent of the entire GCSE.
- You have to do two questions on **Germany** 1918–41 or **Russia** 1916–41 or **United States of America** 1918–39 (only Germany is covered in this book) and two questions on **Britain, Northern Ireland** and **Ireland** (30 minutes for each question).
- Includes short structured answers and extended writing.

Germany c1918–41
Three sections (do **TWO**)

Key Issue 1	The Weimar Republic
Key Issue 2	Nazi Germany
Key Issue 3	Nazi Policy towards Europe

AND

Peace, War and Neutrality: Britain, Northern Ireland and Ireland and the Second World War c1932–49
Three sections (do **TWO**)

Key Issue 1	Anglo-Irish Relationships before World War II
Key Issue 2	Experience of and Response to War
Key Issue 3	Post-War Relationships

OR

Changing Relationships: Britain, Northern Ireland and Ireland c1965–85
Three sections (do **TWO**)

Key Issue 1	Northern Ireland in the 1960s
Key Issue 2	Prelude to Direct Rule
Key Issue 3	Search for a Solution

Paper 2

- Lasts 1 hour 15 minutes.
- Questions only on the Cold War.
- Is worth 30 per cent of the entire GCSE.
- Includes one source question and one two-part essay question.

The Cold War c1945–91
Two sections

- The actions taken by the USSR and USA over the spread of communism in the Far East, and elsewhere 1945–91.

- The attempts by the USSR to keep control, and eventually to relax control of Eastern Europe and the reaction of the USA to this 1945–91.

Section A
Four-part source-based question

Section B
ONE essay from a choice of three

Timing

Getting the timing right in the examination is crucial. You must spend *no more* than the amount of time that I suggest below on each question. Indeed, if possible, try to gain a little extra time in the earlier questions in each section to use on the last question (Question (c)) in each section of Paper 1. That's because these questions are worth the most. If you run out of time on these questions then you run the risk of losing a lot of marks, and this could have a major impact on your overall grade.

Similarly, in Paper 2 spend *no more* than the indicated amount of time on each section. There are too many marks at stake for you to leave yourself short of time when it comes to Question 1 (c) and the essay question that you choose to do in Section B.

The following advice on timing is the author's, not CCEA's.

Germany Paper
Three sections (do **TWO**)

Spend 30 minutes **MAXIMUM** on each section.

Question (a) (i and ii)
◆ 4 marks   4 minutes

Question (b) (i)
◆ 4 marks   5 minutes

Question (b) (ii)
◆ 5 marks   7 minutes

Question (c)
◆ 12 marks   14 minutes

Northern Ireland Papers
Three sections (do **TWO**)

Spend 30 minutes **MAXIMUM** on each section.

Question (a) (i and ii)
◆ 4 marks   4 minutes

Question (b) (i)
◆ 4 marks   5 minutes

Question (b) (ii)
◆ 5 marks   7 minutes

Question (c) (i)
◆ 6 marks   7 minutes

Question (c) (ii)
◆ 6 marks   7 minutes

Cold War Paper
Two sections (do **BOTH**)

Section A
Four-part source-based question – 45 minutes

Question 1 (a)
◆ 4 marks   5 minutes

Question 1 (b)
◆ 6 marks   7.5 minutes

Question 1 (c)
◆ 8 marks   10 minutes

Question 1 (d)
◆ 12 marks   15 minutes

Section B
ONE essay from a choice of three – 30 minutes

Question (a)
◆ 18 marks   22.5 minutes

Question (b)
◆ 12 marks   15 minutes

Grade Boundaries

The grade boundaries change each year. To find out what the grade boundaries were in previous years' examinations look at the Chief Examiner's Reports for History. They can be found on the CCEA website at www.ccea.org.uk.

REVISION TECHNIQUES

Everyone revises differently. For some people, it is a matter of sitting at a desk; for others, pacing up and down. While some people can work with music in the background, others require total silence. The bottom line is, there's no single way!

Whatever your style, there are a number of practical suggestions as to how you should approach revision and use your time.

◆ Start your revision in plenty of time.
◆ Organise a revision timetable for each section of the course.
◆ Draw up a revision checklist that allows you to focus most on the parts of the course that you are most concerned about.
◆ Set yourself a target of material to cover in each session – for example, the impact of the Wall Street Crash – and stick to it.
◆ Revise for short periods – 15–20 minutes for example – and take breaks in-between.
◆ Use the tasks after each section in this book as a way of testing your grasp of the key facts.
◆ Review what you have covered at the end of the day and again the next day to make sure you have internalised the information.
◆ Be open to using a range of ways of remembering material. For example rhymes, mnemonics, coding and diagrams.
◆ Practise questions from past papers to familiarise yourself with the kinds of questions that the examiners set.
◆ Consult CCEA mark schemes and Chief Examiner's Reports to see what the examiners are looking for and – more importantly – what mistakes they want you to avoid.
◆ Leave yourself time to revisit material that you have already revised closer to the time of the examination.

SITTING THE EXAMINATION

I General Points when sitting the examination

- Make sure you're **looking at the right questions**. This is particularly relevant to the two Britain, Northern Ireland and Ireland sections.
- Look for **all of the questions** – some may be over the page. Don't forget to check!
- Follow the **instructions** on the front of the exam paper and within each section.
- **Read** each question – more than once.
- Use a highlighter pen to emphasise **key points** in a question.
- Answer the question that has been set – not the one you wish had been set!
- Stay for the **full amount** of time. You can't get marks if you're not there.

II Specific Papers and Questions

General Points for BOTH Papers

- Remember the connection between the amount of marks for each question and how much you are expected to write.
- Stick rigidly to whatever dates are given in a question. You will get no marks for going beyond the dates given.
- If you want to score strongly in each part of the examination you must spend the appropriate amount of time on each. Too much time spent on one section will meant too little left for others and will cost you significant amounts of marks.

Paper 1 General Points:

Your answers must demonstrate a detailed **knowledge**. This book provides you with the **key facts** on each topic. Learn these thoroughly.

Structure your answer. Most frequently a **chronological framework** will be the best way to achieve this.

Select appropriate **facts** to answer the question asked.

Many pupils lose marks by **failing to identify all relevant information**. Instead of writing a lot about one point, try to write a little about a number of points.

Paper 2 General Points

- Read the sources and the source questions carefully. Use a highlighter pen to underline **key points**.
- Identify all **relevant information** in the sources.
- Ask yourself whether or not the source is providing you with **fact** or **opinion**.
- Use your **own knowledge** to explain the **background** to the source. This will help you to determine its **reliability**.
- Remember to consider what the source **fails to say** as much as what it does – again your own knowledge will be essential here.
- The **reliability** and **bias** of sources must be considered.
- Use the **sources** (whatever ones are specified) in your answers to support what you say when you are instructed to.
- Use your **own knowledge** in your answers to support what you say when you are instructed to.
- As with Paper 1, look for a **number of different points** in your answer. Frequently the examiner will award a mark for each point mentioned up to the maximum available.

TECHNIQUE

Spend **the full amount of time** on each section.

The examiners are looking for you to answer this type of question in a **logical manner**. A good way to approach this question is **chronologically**.

It is important that you **do not** answer the question simply by using each of the three headings provided in the question and writing a short answer on each.

These headings are designed as **prompts** only; you need to **identify and develop the different points** behind each one.

Too much detail will gain no extra **marks**. These questions **do not require explanation**.

You should write a **couple of sentences** on each part of Question (a).

Note **how many marks each question is worth** and spend the **correct amount of time** writing.

These questions require both **analysis and explanation**.

You must make sure that you focus on both the **'how'** and the **'why'** part of the question. Too many students focus only on the 'how' part and lose a lot of marks.

Paper 1   **A1: Germany c1918–41**

Answer any **two** questions

You should spend about 30 minutes on each question

1. **This question is about the Weimar Republic**
   (a) (i)   Write down two examples of how the hyperinflation crisis of 1923 affected Germany.
       (ii) Give two measures taken by Stresemann to solve the hyperinflation crisis of 1923.
                                                                        [4]
   (b) Between 1923 and 1929 the Nazis tried to gain power in Germany.
       (i)   How did the Nazis try to seize power in 1923?
                                                                        [4]
       (ii) How did the Nazis change their tactics between 1924 and 1929?
                                                                        [5]
   (c) Why and how did the Weimar Republic collapse in 1933?
       Use the following to explain your answer:
       • weaknesses of the Weimar Government;
       • economic problems;
       • growth of extremist parties.
                                                                        [12]

TECHNIQUE

Here the examiners are looking for you to provide roughly **FOUR** pieces of information from the indicated source that tell you something about the focus of the question. Remember that this is a **straightforward comprehension question** that requires you to provide **no contextual/background knowledge**. You don't need to write more than a paragraph to answer this question.

This is the kind of question that can cause a lot of problems. Remember that you are being asked to consider **TWO** things:

1. How **USEFUL** the source is.

Useful means **what do you learn from the source**, what does it tell you. Most importantly, remember to comment – considering your own knowledge – on what the source does **NOT** tell us.

2. How **RELIABLE** the source is.

Reliability means **whether or not we can take what it says to be true**. When discussing reliability the issue of **bias** will more than likely appear. Remember, just because a source is biased – and all sources are biased in some way or other – does not mean that it is not useful. **ALL sources are useful for what they tell us about how a person or group was thinking**.

Remember, you must cover **BOTH** reliability and utility if you want to gain top marks.

Paper 2   Section A

1. This section is about the Vietnam War.

(a) Study Source A.

What does Source A tell us about the problems faced by the US Army in the Vietnam War?

[4]

(b) Study Sources B and C.

How far do Sources B and C agree in explaining the role of the USA in the Vietnam War?

[6]

(c) Study Source D.

How reliable and useful is Source D in explaining the attitudes of the American public to the Vietnam War?

[8]

(d) Study Sources A, B and C.

Source B says that the American Government believed "that in Vietnam, they were waging a just war against the Vietcong, a Communist movement led from North Vietnam."

Using Sources A, B and C and your own knowledge explain whether or not you think this is a fair interpretation of American involvement in the Vietnam War.

[12]

This type of question can be awkward if you don't **structure your answer carefully**. The first thing to do is **identify the relevant points** in the first source and then **look for similar points in the second source**. However, if you want to aim for the top marks you must also **indicate the areas where the two sources do NOT agree**. You should identify these points as you go through each source.

The key point here is to remember to **use BOTH the sources AND your own knowledge**. First of all the sources will more than likely present you with **a range of interpretations** about an event. You need to be able to **identify these different viewpoints and explain why they are different**. It is your own knowledge that will enable you to judge whether or not the interpretation is valid. In all likelihood there will be points you will make from the sources and your own knowledge that **support the quotation**. Equally there will be points that you can include to make that **disprove the quotation**. Make sure that your answer **reflects these different viewpoints**. In the end, remember to **come to a conclusion**!

HOW TO APPROACH SOURCES

As you look at the different kinds of sources you might encounter, consider some of the following ideas to try and improve the quality of your answer.

Written Sources

Primary Sources A primary source is one that dates from the time of the event.

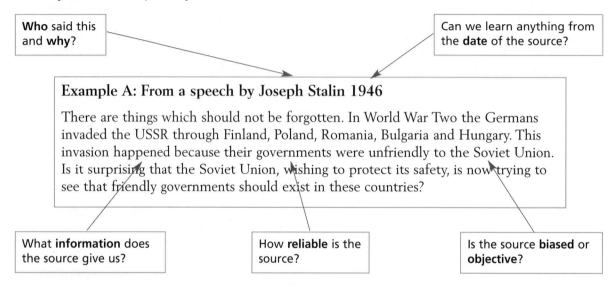

> Who said this and why?
>
> Can we learn anything from the date of the source?
>
> **Example A: From a speech by Joseph Stalin 1946**
>
> There are things which should not be forgotten. In World War Two the Germans invaded the USSR through Finland, Poland, Romania, Bulgaria and Hungary. This invasion happened because their governments were unfriendly to the Soviet Union. Is it surprising that the Soviet Union, wishing to protect its safety, is now trying to see that friendly governments should exist in these countries?
>
> What **information** does the source give us?
>
> How **reliable** is the source?
>
> Is the source **biased** or **objective**?

Secondary Sources A secondary source usually comes from a time after the event being written about.

Newspapers

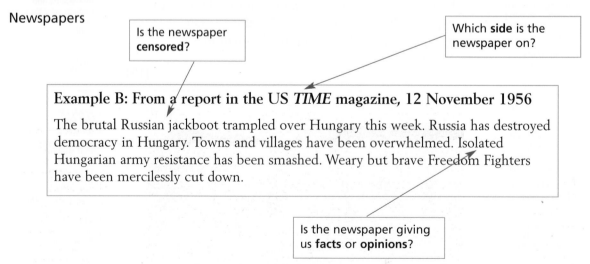

> Is the newspaper **censored**?
>
> Which **side** is the newspaper on?
>
> **Example B: From a report in the US *TIME* magazine, 12 November 1956**
>
> The brutal Russian jackboot trampled over Hungary this week. Russia has destroyed democracy in Hungary. Towns and villages have been overwhelmed. Isolated Hungarian army resistance has been smashed. Weary but brave Freedom Fighters have been mercilessly cut down.
>
> Is the newspaper giving us **facts** or **opinions**?

Historians' Accounts

What **side** – if any – is the historian likely to be on?

What **information** does the source contain? Does it seem **reasonable/accurate**?

Example C: John Terraine British historian 1974

The East German Government tried to prevent their people escaping from their 'workers' paradise' by walling them in. There were awful scenes when the Wall was erected in Berlin with people flinging themselves out of high windows and crashing to their deaths. The Wall and frontier fence have so far claimed over 170 victims.

Is the account likely to be **censored**?

Photographic Evidence

We expect photographs to be reliable, but this is not always the case. When you get a photograph as a source you should ask yourself the following questions about it.

Can we **trust** the caption?

Which **side** is the photographer on? Does the photograph tell us?

Is the photograph **propaganda**? Is it **biased**?

Example D: Photograph taken in Prague in 1968

Czechs shout at Soviet soldiers on the streets of Prague.

Is the photograph **genuine** or **faked**?

Does the photograph **tell us everything** about the situation? Does it tell us what happened just before, or after this photograph was taken? Does this tell us how **ALL** Czechs felt? Were other Czechs cheering the Russian soldiers?

Essay Questions

◆ Spend at least **30 minutes** on the essay question in Section B of Paper 2.
◆ Look carefully at the question. Make sure you read it all and don't just focus on one word or phrase. Check out the dates that the question requires you to cover. Do not go beyond these dates.
◆ Use **key words** from the questions to help you structure your answer.
◆ Spend a few minutes jotting down an essay plan that will bring the examiner through the topic in a logical manner.
◆ **Structure** your answer. Use **paragraphs** (and again most likely a **chronological framework**).
◆ **Refer to the question frequently** throughout your answer and avoid narrative.
◆ Put in **relevant information** only. An essay on the development of the Cold War in Europe 1945–68 does not require any analysis of China, Korea, Cuba or Vietnam!
◆ Keep the two parts of your essay **separate**. It makes it easier for the examiner to mark them properly.
◆ Remember that you are being asked to **come to a conclusion**, not simply list all of the facts that you think are relevant to the issue.

Chapter 2　GERMANY c1918–41

Section 1　The Weimar Republic

GERMANY BEFORE 1918

> **A bit of background**
> *This first bit isn't directly asked about in the GCSE exam. However, it's useful to know in terms of setting the scene.*

Before 1871 Germany was not one country but a number of individual states. In 1871 it was unified under the leadership of Prussia, the largest and most powerful state. The new country was ruled by the Prussian King who was given the title of **Kaiser**.

The Kaiser wanted Germany to be Europe's most powerful state and so the country developed both economically and militarily. However, all of this growth came at a price. Germany's aggressive policies annoyed France, Russia and Britain. By August 1914 tensions were so bad that war broke out between these nations.

> ## Germany in 1918 (I) *WHAT YOU NEED TO KNOW*
>
> *Here's where your knowledge really needs to start. You need to understand <u>how</u> and <u>why</u> Germans' attitudes to the war changed and <u>how</u> this impacted on the Kaiser.*

Impact of the War

Initially Germans welcomed the war, but discontent soon emerged due to increasing food shortages and a decline in the value of currency. During 1918 hundreds of thousands of Germans died during a 'flu pandemic.

Although the people were being told that the war was going well, by October 1918 the German Government knew that defeat was inevitable. The army was exhausted and soldiers were deserting.

The Kaiser was persuaded to made Germany into a **constitutional monarchy** as:

1. It was felt that a civilian government would obtain fairer peace terms from the **Allies**;
2. It was believed that the new Government would get the blame for ending the war, allowing the army to accuse it of stabbing them in the back.

Tasks

1. Fill in the following table:

The impact of the war at home	
The changes made to Germany's government	
Why these changes were made	

Germany in 1918 (II) *WHAT YOU NEED TO KNOW*

So how was the Kaiser kicked out? This section explains <u>why</u> he left and <u>how</u> people reacted. Make sure that you are clear about <u>all of the changes</u> that took place.

Abdication

On 3 November 1918, a naval revolt broke out at Kiel. Local workers joined in and the protest spread with Russian-style workers' councils being set up. Within a week Berlin was paralysed by a general strike while communist **republics** were set up in Saxony and Bavaria.

With Germany facing revolution the Kaiser was persuaded to **abdicate**. He did so on 9 November 1918 and was replaced by the Social Democrat Party (SDP) leader Friedrich Ebert who declared Germany a republic. On 11 November 1918, Germany signed an **armistice** that brought the fighting in the war to an end.

These events shocked most ordinary Germans who had been led to believe that the war was going well. Their anger was directed towards the new Government – just as the Kaiser and army had intended.

Tasks

1. Complete the following mix and match activity:

Date	Event
November 3	Germany declared a Republic
November 9	Naval Revolt
November 11	Ebert becomes leader of Germany
	Kaiser abdicates

2. Complete the following table:

Reasons for Kaiser's abdication	
Why most Germans were shocked by the armistice	
Impact defeat had on attitudes towards Germany's new leaders	

Threat from the Left *WHAT YOU NEED TO KNOW*

There were many different political viewpoints in Germany. You need to understand the difference between left wing and right wing as well as <u>how</u> and <u>why</u> some on the left wing wanted to overthrow Ebert's Government.

Political Divisions

The terms left wing and right wing are used to describe different political viewpoints. Put simply, left wing refers to people who want radical change while right wing refers to people who are against change. There were plenty of both in Germany!

The Spartacists

Ebert faced particular opposition from the left-wing Spartacists, led by Rosa Luxemburg and Karl Liebknecht. They wanted Russian-style workers' councils to run Germany. On 6 January 1919, the Spartacists – now calling themselves the German Communist Party (KPD) – launched a rising or *putsch* against the new SPD Government. It was unlikely to succeed, though, as it was poorly equipped, badly organised and lacked widespread support.

The *putsch* was crushed by the army supported by the Free Corps, a right-wing volunteer army made up mainly of former soldiers who detested communism. By 15 January 1919, the rising was over and both Spartacist leaders had been murdered.

Further Unrest

Over the next few months the left wing posed further challenges:

1. In March 1919 Berlin was the scene of further communist unrest. Again the Free Corps was called upon to act; again they destroyed the opposition.
2. In the same month a Soviet Republic was declared in Bavaria. In response, the Weimar Government besieged Munich, the state capital, finally taking control on 1 May.

Tasks

1. Consider which of the following statements are TRUE and which are FALSE:

	SPD	KPD
Left-wing party		
Supported **democracy**		
Believed in using violence		
Led by Ebert		
Led by Liebknecht and Luxemburg		

2. Fill in the following table:

Example of left-wing opposition	Date	Location	Outcome

Establishing a **New System** *WHAT YOU NEED TO KNOW*

One area of confusion for students is the Weimar Constitution. You need to understand <u>how</u> the system established worked, <u>what</u> its strengths were and – most importantly – <u>how</u> its weaknesses might cause problems in the future.

A New Constitution

Elections for the new German Parliament were held in January 1919. The Social Democrats won the most seats and in February 1919, Ebert was elected President of the new German Republic.

The first task was to draw up a **constitution**. As there was too much unrest in Berlin, the politicians moved to the quieter town of Weimar. Thus Germany became known as the Weimar Republic.

The constitution made Germany the most democratic country in the world but some of its strengths would also turn out to be weaknesses.

Part of constitution	Reasons why it was a strength	Reasons why it was a weakness
Proportional representation used for elections (every four years).	This gave all parties the chance of winning seats in parliament.	More parties in parliament made it harder for the bigger parties to win a majority. This usually meant that governments were made up of a number of parties (**coalitions**) who could fall out quite easily, making laws difficult to pass. This could undermine democracy.
In a political crisis when the government could not get enough support from parliament, Article 48 allowed the President to rule using emergency decrees.	This meant that the country could still be governed even in a crisis.	Using Article 48 meant that the elected Government was not running the country, which was undemocratic.

To make matters worse the army, **civil service** and **judiciary** were carried over largely unchanged from the old system. They remained lukewarm at best and openly hostile at worst in their attitude towards the Weimar Republic.

Tasks

1. Complete the table by ticking or writing as appropriate:

Outcome	Proportional representation	Article 48	Strength or weakness?
Allows more parties to get seats in parliament.			
Allows the President to pass laws.			
Can result in too many parties getting into parliament, making it difficult to set up a strong government.			
Means the country can still be run without parliament.			
Multi-party governments can fall out easily when it can't agree on policy.			
Running the country without parliament can be undemocratic.			
Means that governments are usually made up of a number of parties.			

2. Fill in the following table:

Group opposed to Weimar	Why this mattered
Army	
Civil service	
Judiciary	

The Treaty of Versailles *WHAT YOU NEED TO KNOW*

The new Government was already unpopular because it had ended the war even though it had no choice. Signing the Treaty of Versailles – again even though it had no choice – increased its unpopularity.

Key Terms

The Allies spent the early part of 1919 drawing up the peace treaties that would officially end World War I. Having been excluded from the negotiations, the German delegation was shown the Treaty on 7 May 1919. There were three main parts:

1. **Land**
   Germany lost land to France, Belgium and Poland; the latter via the Polish Corridor which split Germany in two. Any union (*anschluss*) with Austria was forbidden. She also lost her overseas colonies. In a number of disputed regions, such as Schleswig, Allenstein, Marienwerder and Silesia, the Allies organised **plebiscites**. In total, Germany lost 13 per cent of her land, 12 per cent of her population, 15 per cent of her agricultural production, 16 per cent of her coal production and 48 per cent of her iron production.

2. **Arms**
   To stop Germany going to war again, particularly against France, the Rhineland was **demilitarised** and occupied by the Allies for 15 years. The army was restricted to 100,000 men and conscription was prohibited. The navy was limited to six battleships while submarines and an air force were banned.

3. **War guilt and reparations**
   According to Article 231 of the Treaty, Germany had to accept all blame for causing the war. On the basis of this guilt, Germany had to compensate the Allies for war damages (**reparations**). The figure for this would be agreed at a later date.

Reactions

Despite German outrage, the Allies refused to change the terms of the settlement and, faced with the threat of renewed war, Ebert instructed the German delegation to sign the Treaty. They did so in the Palace of Versailles on 28 June 1919.

Given the significant political changes that had been made, Germans had been expecting a just settlement. They were outraged by the Treaty, which they christened a *diktat* (dictated peace). They turned on the Weimar politicians who had signed the armistice in November 1918 that had ended the fighting and had led to the Treaty. They argued that these politicians had betrayed Germany and began calling them 'November criminals'. Although this charge was untrue, from that point on the new Republic became associated in the eyes of many people with betrayal and defeat.

Task

1. Create a spider diagram listing the key terms of Versailles under the headings of (i) Land, (ii) Military and (iii) War guilt.

2004 Past Paper and Mark Scheme

(a) (i) Give **two** terms of the Treaty of Versailles.

(ii) Give **two** reasons why the Treaty of Versailles was unpopular with many Germans.

[4]

(a) (i) Your answer could include any two of the following:
- loss of land, especially in the east to Poland. Germany was now divided;
- economic loss;
- army limited to 100,000: restrictions on navy; no air force allowed;
- Article 231 War Guilt Clause accepted blame for war. This led to reparations.

(ii) Your answer could include any two of the following:
- right-wing groups, especially the army and elite, blamed the Weimar politicians for signing the treaty. They were 'the November criminals' who 'stabbed the German army in the back';
- bitterness at loss of land in the east. Loss of millions of Germans in West Prussia to Poland;
- reparations were set too high. These placed an excessive economic burden on Germany whose economy had suffered much damage in World War I;
- Versailles was seen as a '*diktat*', a settlement imposed in Germany.

Threats from the Right WHAT YOU NEED TO KNOW

We've already seen the different ways in which the left wing tried to destroy the new Republic. Now it was the turn of the right. What is important for you to understand is how the army reacted to the rising.

The Kapp *Putsch*

On 13 March 1920, the Free Corps – led by Wolfgang Kapp – seized key locations in Berlin. The immediate cause was anger at the reduction in the size of the army as demanded by the Treaty of Versailles.

Ebert ordered the army to take action but it refused and the government was forced to flee. However, workers in Berlin and elsewhere did not support the *putsch* and organised a general strike. Within four days Berlin was at a standstill and Kapp was forced to flee. While Ebert was undoubtedly pleased with the failure of the *putsch* he had much to be concerned about in terms of the reaction of the military to this threat. Despite this, the Government took no action against the army.

Assassinations

The danger from the right wing was also evident from the assassination of Foreign Minister Walter Rathenau in 1922. Like so many of the murders carried out by elements of the right, during the period 1920–2, punishments were light if there were any at all. Similar crimes carried out by those on the left were invariably dealt with more harshly.

Task

1. Fill in the following information about the Kapp *Putsch*:

Reasons	Events	Results

More Unrest *WHAT YOU NEED TO KNOW*

The left challenged the government again. What is interesting is <u>how</u> the Republic still relied on the unreliable Free Corps to save it.

'Red Rising'

No sooner had the Kapp *Putsch* ended than the Government faced another threat. This time the danger came from communist workers in the Ruhr, Germany's industrial heartland. In reaction to the Kapp *Putsch* they had gone on strike. However, even though the *putsch* was over they stayed on strike. Their aim was to obtain concessions from the Government they had just saved.

This 'Red Rising' was put down by government troops supported by some of the same Free Corps who had just tried to seize power.

The events of March 1920 clearly demonstrated the weakness of the Weimar Government's position. It had to rely on a group of right-wing extremists to keep it in power, but these same extremists were willing to overthrow the Government given half a chance.

Task

1. Fill in the following information about the 'Red Rising':

Reasons	Events	Results

2. Complete the following table:

Group	Ruhr workers	Free Corps
Reasons why government should have trusted them		
Reasons why government should not have trusted them		

The 1923 Economic Crisis (I) The Problem *WHAT YOU NEED TO KNOW*

This is one of the hardest parts of the course to understand and it appears in the exam regularly. The important thing to understand is <u>why</u> the crisis developed, <u>how</u> the Government responded, <u>what</u> it meant for the economy and <u>how</u> it affected ordinary Germans.

Reparations

In January 1921 the Allies announced that Germany would have to pay £6,600 million in reparations. Germany managed to pay the first instalments; then in December 1922 it announced that it would not be able to meet the next payment and asked for a break.

Thinking that Germany was trying to get off paying reparations, the French refused to agree. In January 1923 French and Belgian troops invaded the Ruhr – Germany's industrial heartland – with the aim of taking what they were owed.

The Government responded by ordering the population of the Ruhr to engage in **passive resistance**. This made Germany's economic problems even worse:

1. The richest part of the country was not producing anything, thus reducing the country's income;
2. The government had to start importing the goods not being producing, costing more money;
3. The Ruhr workers still had to be paid even though they were not working.

Hyperinflation

The government's solution was to print more and more money, and by the autumn of 1923 Germany was experiencing **hyperinflation**. Particularly affected were the poor who had nothing and the middle classes whose savings were wiped out by hyperinflation. With money worthless, Germany developed into a **barter economy**.

Not everyone suffered. Those whose wealth was not in money were unaffected, while some people were able to pay off various kinds of loans cheaply.

Tasks

1. Explain the crisis using the headings of (i) Reasons and (ii) Results.

2. Complete the following table:

Groups most affected by the hyperinflation crisis	Groups least affected by the hyperinflation crisis

The 1923 Economic Crisis (II) The Solution *WHAT YOU NEED TO KNOW*

Once you get to grips with how the crisis started, your next task is to understand <u>what</u> the government did to end it.

In August 1923, Gustav Stresemann became Chancellor. He ended the crisis by:

◆ ordering an end to passive resistance to start the economy working again
◆ sharply reducing government spending
◆ agreeing to resume paying reparations, realising that this was the only way to get the French and Belgians out of the Ruhr
◆ announcing, in November 1923, the establishment of a new national bank and the introduction of a new currency, the Rentenmark.

While Stresemann's actions restored economic stability, the 1923 crisis damaged the faith of many – particularly those in the middle class – in the Weimar Republic.

Tasks

1. Create a spider diagram illustrating Stresemann's solutions to the 1923 crisis.

2004 Past Paper and Mark Scheme

(a) In 1923 Germany experienced hyperinflation.
   (i) How did the hyperinflation crisis of 1923 affect life in Germany?

   [4]
   (ii) How did the Weimar Government deal with the problem of hyperinflation between 1923 and 1924?

   [5]

(a) (i) Reference should be made to some of the following:
   - Passive resistance led to the Weimar Government paying millions of marks to those who lost wages. At the same time government revenue fell.
   - Printing of money led to a collapse of confidence in the mark and the German financial system.
   - People on fixed income and pensions faced great hardship as they were unable to purchase goods at inflated prices.
   - Savings became worthless. This hit the middle classes.
   - Those who had loans and mortgages or a fixed rent benefited as inflation increased.

   (ii) Reference should be made to some of the following:
   - New government led by Stresemann took measures to end the hyperinflation crisis. Passive resistance was called off and French and Belgian troops withdrew.
   - September 1923 the repayment of reparations resumed.
   - November 1923 a new currency, the Rentenmark.
   - 1924 Germany's reparations were restructured with international help.

Recovery *WHAT YOU NEED TO KNOW*

Stresemann moved to ensure that Germany stabilised economically and began to get on with her former enemies again. You need to be aware of the agreements he made to achieve this.

In 1924 Stresemann and key Allied leaders produced the Dawes Plan. This allowed Germany to pay a reduced amount of reparations for several years, with longer to pay overall. However, the total amount remained the same at £6,600 million. Large loans – mainly American – were also promised to help rebuild the German economy.

Further help with reparations came in the shape of the 1929 Young Plan. This reduced the amount Germany would have to pay to £1,800 million and gave even longer to pay it.

In 1925 Stresemann signed the Locarno Treaty in which Germany, France and Belgium agreed to accept their common borders. Shortly after this, French and Belgian troops withdrew from the Ruhr. A year later, Germany was finally allowed to join the **League of Nations**.

Tasks

1. Complete the following mix and match activity:

Date		Event
1924		Germany joins League of Nations
1925		Young Plan
1926		Locarno Treaty
1929		Dawes Plan

2. Complete the following table:

	Dawes Plan	Young Plan
Date agreed		
Reparations total (£)		
Longer to pay? (Circle)	Yes / No	Yes / No

The 'Golden Twenties'? *WHAT YOU NEED TO KNOW*

This period can sometimes confuse students. On the surface, Germany appeared to be working well both economically and politically; however, beneath the surface, the picture was very different.

The Positive

On the surface, it seemed as if Stresemann had restored Germany's prosperity and economic confidence. Heavy industry recovered, exports rose, social welfare provision improved and infrastructure was developed. Moreover there were no more *putsches,* while the results of the 1928 **general election** indicated that people were supporting moderate rather than extremist parties. The same election resulted in the establishment of the stable Grand Coalition.

The Negative

However, much of this stability was misleading. The anti-democratic Paul von Hindenburg was elected President in 1925. Parties were getting on better because there was nothing significant for them to fall out over. At the same time, industry was growing unsteadily, agriculture was in a depression, unemployment was on the increase, welfare costs were up and the Government was spending more than it was making.

The biggest weakness, however, was Germany's over-reliance on the loans she was receiving from the USA.

Tasks

1. Complete the following tables comparing good and bad points of the 'Golden Twenties':

Political	
Reasons why the twenties were golden	Reasons why the twenties were not golden

Economic	
Reasons why the twenties were golden	Reasons why the twenties were not golden

Hitler and the Origins of Nazi Party *WHAT YOU NEED TO KNOW*

You should know about Hitler's early life just for context. It is <u>how</u> he got involved with the German Workers' Party and <u>what</u> their policies were that is essential knowledge for you.

Early Life

Adolf Hitler was born in Austria in 1889. In 1913 he went to Germany to avoid conscription. When war broke out in 1914 he joined the German army. When the conflict ended in 1918, Hitler was in hospital. He was inconsolable when he learned that Germany's leaders had signed an armistice.

On his release from hospital, Hitler remained in the army. In his new role of political spy, he was asked to investigate the German Workers' Party (DAP), an extreme nationalist party that had been set up by Anton Drexler. After attending a meeting, Hitler joined the party.

The Nazi Party

Hitler's influence over the party was immediate. In February 1920 a new party manifesto, the 25 Point Programme, was announced. The programme – most of which was Hitler's work – outlined a range of key ideas:

- destruction of the Treaty of Versailles
- the need for *lebensraum* (living space)
- the need for strong government
- the desire to unite all Germans, whilst excluding the Jews.

At the same time, the DAP was renamed the National Socialist German Workers' Party (NSDAP, or Nazi for short).

In July 1921 Hitler replaced Drexler as Nazi leader after threatening to resign from the party. A month later the Sturmabteilung (SA) was set up as the Nazis' paramilitary wing. Many of its recruits came from the now-dissolved Free Corps. They were known as the brownshirts because of their uniforms.

Tasks

1. Create a timeline of Hitler's life from 1889 to 1921.

2. Create a spider diagram illustrating the key points about the DAP/NSDAP.

The Munich *Putsch* WHAT YOU NEED TO KNOW

The Munich Putsch was the last attempt by any group to overthrow the Weimar Republic by force. You need to understand <u>what</u> Hitler was trying to do, <u>how</u> it all went wrong and <u>why</u> he got off so lightly.

Plans

By November 1923 Germany was in crisis. Hitler had been particularly angered at Stresemann's decision to call off passive resistance. He saw this as yet another example of the kind of cowardice that had led to the signing of the armistice.

Hitler hoped to exploit the Republic's problems by seizing power in Munich, before marching on to Berlin. On the evening of 8 November 1923, he interrupted a meeting being held by Gustav von Kahr and Otto von Lossow, the leaders of the Bavarian Government and army. They were forced to support Hitler's plan. The First World War hero General Ludendorff also supported the intended *putsch*. Hitler hoped that Ludendorff's involvement would secure the backing of the local army and police.

Failure

However, Hitler's plans went badly wrong. The Bavarian government leaders ordered the army to stop the intended *putsch*. As over 2000 Nazis marched towards the centre of Munich, armed police opened fire, killing sixteen. Hitler and Ludendorff were arrested and charged with high treason.

Hitler appeared to be finished. However, he turned his trial to his advantage, using it to condemn the Weimar Republic and to spread his ideas. The media coverage provided Hitler with more publicity than he could ever have dreamt of.

This wasn't the only stroke of luck he enjoyed; the trial judges were sympathetic and at the end of the trial he was sentenced to just five years in jail. Ludendorff was freed.

Task

1. Fill in the following information about the Munich *Putsch*:

Reasons	Planning	Events (timeline)	Results

Nazi Reorganisation and Growth *WHAT YOU NEED TO KNOW*

It is essential that you understand <u>how</u> Hitler's experience in 1923 made him realise that he had to change tactics if he was to gain power. You should also be aware of <u>how</u> he reorganised the Nazi Party and <u>why</u> his changes had no effect in 1928.

New Tactics

Hitler only served nine months in prison. He used his time there to write down his ideas in *Mein Kampf* (My Struggle). He also decided that instead of using force to overthrow the Weimar Republic, the Nazis would use the political system. Once in control, they could then destroy the Republic.

After his release in December 1924, Hitler refounded the Nazi Party and organised it across Germany. It now stressed complete obedience to Hitler (**Führerprinzip**). New groups were established including the SS in 1925 and the Hitler Youth in 1926.

1928 Election

The reorganised party's first electoral test came in 1928: it won only twelve seats. Apart from this being a time when extremist parties did poorly, as Weimar appeared to be stable and prosperous, people were still not taking the party seriously.

Tasks

1. Create a timeline showing the key developments in Hitler's life from 1923 to 1928.
2. Create a spider diagram explaining the reasons why the Nazis performed poorly in the 1928 general election.

Germany and the Great Depression *WHAT YOU NEED TO KNOW*

The period covering the Great Depression is the most complicated part of the course. To start off you need to understand <u>how</u> the Wall Street Crash impacted on Germany politically and economically.

Economic Collapse

In October 1929 two disasters befell the Weimar Republic:

1. Gustav Stresemann died.
2. The US economy collapsed with the Wall Street Crash. American investors demanded immediate repayment of all loans.

Germany's economy collapsed. Prices and wages fell, businesses went bankrupt as demand for their products stopped and thousands lost their jobs. By the winter of 1929–30, unemployment stood at over two million. By September 1930, over three million Germans were unemployed while banks were closing their doors, resulting in a loss of savings for millions.

Political Collapse

Faced with such a range of problems, the Government began to break up and in March 1930 Chancellor Müller resigned. Heinrich Brüning of the Centre Party took over but still the Government remained divided. The largest party, the Social Democrats, rejected the demands of other coalition parties to cut welfare benefits. When the Reichstag rejected a budget that proposed to increase taxes and slash government spending, a General Election was called for in September 1930.

In this election, the Nazis and Communists increased their support with the former winning 107 seats and the latter 77. All of the moderate parties lost support.

Brüning remained as Chancellor despite being unable to form a stable government. Unable to get parliament to agree to his laws, he was forced to ask Hindenburg to pass laws using Article 48. For the next two years all key laws were passed in this way; democracy was undermined.

Tasks

1. Create two spider diagrams showing the political and economic impacts of the Wall Street Crash.
2. Explain how the following elements of the Weimar Constitution undermined democracy in Germany at this time:

	Proportional representation	Article 48
How it was meant to work		
How it was working in Germany in 1930		
The implications for democracy		

Brüning's Government *WHAT YOU NEED TO KNOW*

Brüning was Chancellor from 1930 to 1932. His policies had an important effect on the growth of the Nazis. His successor, von Papen, also played a key part in the eventual rise of Hitler. You need to know as much as possible about the <u>policies</u> followed by both Chancellors.

'Hunger Chancellor'

In order to avoid hyperinflation, Brüning introduced harsh economic policies. He:

◆ reduced public spending
◆ imposed tariffs on imports
◆ slashed unemployment benefits
◆ introduced wage cuts for civil servants.

Brüning's policies were very unpopular and they earned him the nickname of 'Hunger Chancellor'. However, by late 1932 there were some signs of recovery even though unemployment stood at six million. Brüning also managed to get reparations stopped completely in the same year.

In March and April 1932, elections were held for President. Hitler decided to stand, and in the first round of the election received over 30 per cent of the vote. Hindenburg received just under the 50 per cent needed to win, so a second round was needed. This time, although Hitler increased his vote, Hindenburg was re-elected.

Not long after this, Hindenburg forced Brüning to resign by telling him that he would not allow him to use Article 48 any more. The immediate cause of his resignation was two actions taken by the Chancellor:

1. In April 1932 Brüning banned the SA and SS in response to high levels of violence. This concerned General von Schleicher, an influential adviser of Hindenburg. He believed that the time had come to co-operate with the Nazis.
2. Brüning's plan to break up the large estates in Prussia, Hindenburg's home state, was too close to socialism for the President's liking.

Von Papen

On von Schleicher's advice, Hindenburg appointed the Centre Party's Franz von Papen as Chancellor. He removed the ban on the SS and SA, deposed the socialist Government in Prussia and called a general election for July 1932. Again, the only parties who gained support were those opposed to democracy. The Nazis became the largest party with 230 seats.

Tasks

1. Create a spider diagram illustrating Brüning's economic policies, 1930–2.
2. Create a timeline showing the key political developments, 1930–2.
3. Complete the following table:

	Brüning
Party	
Date of appointment	
Reasons for appointment	
Date of dismissal	
Reasons for dismissal	

Why did Support for Nazism Increase? *WHAT YOU NEED TO KNOW*

Examiners will expect you to be able to <u>identify</u> and <u>explain</u> the different reasons for the Nazis' growth in popularity.

Apart from the general political and economic situation, there were several specific reasons why Nazi support increased:

◆ Under the direction of Joseph Göbbels, the Nazis used sophisticated propaganda to win support. Hitler's image and ideas were plastered across Germany.
◆ Nazi groups such as the SA and Hitler Youth won new supporters.
◆ The SA attacked opponents and disrupted their meetings.
◆ Hitler was a gifted speaker who portrayed an image of strength.
◆ Nazi policies focused on the groups who had been hardest hit by the Depression, such as the middle classes, farmers and young people:
  – To those who were starving, homeless, unemployed or had lost their businesses, the Nazis promised jobs and the restoration of a vibrant economy. The key phrase used was 'Bread and work'.
  – To those angry at Germany's military weakness, Hitler offered the overthrow of Versailles and a return to greatness.
◆ Many Germans, particularly leading industrialists such as Krupps and Thyssen, feared the growth of Communism. They were willing to support the Nazis financially, in return for promises from Hitler to smash the trade unions when he gained power.

However, there were a number of groups unlikely to ever support the Nazis:

◆ Trade unions disliked them because the Nazis were keen to close them down.
◆ The movement's lack of discipline resulted in a lack of support from some key industrial figures.
◆ Church leaders disliked them because they threatened Christian values.
◆ The anti-feminist nature of Nazi policies lost them the support of some female voters.

Tasks

1. Create a spider diagram summarising the different reasons for the growth in Nazi support.
2. Create a spider diagram illustrating the groups unlikely ever to vote for the Nazis.

> ## Hitler's Rise to Power *WHAT YOU NEED TO KNOW*
>
> *This is a confusing period. Between July 1932 and January 1933 there were three different chancellors, another General Election and an awful lot of behind-the-door scheming. You must be clear about all of this to understand how Hitler eventually became Chancellor.*

Two Elections

After the July 1932 election, Hitler demanded the Chancellorship. Hindenburg refused and reappointed von Papen. However, his Government lacked support and he decided to call another election.

The results of the November 1932 general election revealed a drop in support for the Nazis (196 seats) although the Communist vote increased (100 seats). Hitler again requested the position of Chancellor. Again Hindenburg refused. Von Papen wanted to stay on and planned to replace the Reichstag and introduce a dictatorial constitution. However, von Schleicher advised the President that such plans risked **civil war**.

Intrigue

Hindenburg now asked von Schleicher to take on the job himself. He only lasted for 57 days, failing in his attempts to strike a deal with the Nazis and incurring Hindenburg's displeasure for requesting the use of Article 48.

Meanwhile, others were trying to persuade Hindenburg to appoint Hitler as Chancellor. Particularly involved in this was von Papen. He negotiated a deal with Hitler whereby he agreed to support Hitler as Chancellor in return for becoming his deputy. Von Papen then convinced Hindenburg to appoint Hitler, assuring the President that he would be able to keep the Nazis under control. On 30 January 1933, Hindenburg finally asked Hitler to take on the job.

Tasks

1. Create a timeline showing the key political developments, 1932-3.
2. Complete the following table:

	von Papen	von Schleicher	Hitler
Party			
Date of appointment			
Reasons for appointment			
Date of dismissal			
Reasons for dismissal			

2004 Past Paper and Mark Scheme

(c) Explain how and why Adolf Hitler was able to become Chancellor of Germany in January 1933.

Use the following to explain your answer:
- Effects of the Wall Street Crash.
- Policies of Hitler and the Nazi Party.
- Weaknesses of the Weimar Government.

[12]

(c) Reference should be made to some of the following:

Guideline 1: Effects of the Wall Street Crash
- German economy was dependent on loans from USA banks. Recall of these loans had a negative effect.
- Collapse of the German banking system in 1931. Millions lost their savings.
- Increase in poverty and unemployment. Six million unemployed by 1932. Sense of despair felt by many Germans.
- Break-up of the Grand Coalition in 1930 over the issue of cutbacks in government spending.

Guideline 2: Policies of Hitler and the Nazi Party
- Hitler and the Nazis used the legal way to increase their influence.
- Hitler's personality and opportunism enabled the Nazis to exploit the effects of the Depression. The slogan 'Bread and work' was attractive to the unemployed.
- Göbbels used propaganda and focused on the grievances of the unemployed, the farmers, the elite.
- Hitler promised to restore German greatness and destroy Versailles.
- Electoral success in Reichstag elections in 1930 and 1932.

Guideline 3: Weakness of the Weimar Government
- Brüning's government lacked solutions to the economic crisis. His main focus was to use the crisis to remove reparations repayments. He was the 'Hunger Chancellor' who cut unemployment benefit and the salaries of civil servants.
- Brüning's government used Article 48 to rule by decree. Laws were passed without the approval of the Reichstag. This weakened the system of democracy.
- Political intrigue in 1932 and early 1933 involving von Papen, von Schleicher and Hindenburg weakened the Weimar Government. The right-wing elite wanted a more authoritarian government. Von Papen was confident he could control Hitler and the Nazis.

Section 2 Nazi Germany

Nazi Consolidation of Power (I) *WHAT YOU NEED TO KNOW*

You need to be able to identify the obstacles to Hitler's achievement of dictatorship and <u>what</u> he did in 1933 to overcome them.

Reichstag Fire

Hitler moved almost immediately to gain an overall majority in the Reichstag, calling fresh elections for 5 March 1933. The burning of the Reichstag building on 27 February gave him the opportunity to weaken the Communists' election campaign. Because a Dutch communist – Marinus van der Lubbe – was captured at the scene, the Nazis blamed the Communists for the blaze. However there remained the suspicion that the Nazis were involved.

Hitler used the fire to exploit Hindenburg's fear of a communist takeover, persuading him to approve the decree *For the Protection of People and State*. This gave the government the power to suspend many civil rights. It violently disrupted the election campaigns of opposition parties and intimidated voters.

Despite their advantages, the Nazis failed to win an overall majority in the Reichstag, winning 288 seats. However, with the support of the Nationalist Party, the Nazis could now count on just over 50 per cent of the votes in the Reichstag. This left Hitler in a stronger position within the coalition and the cabinet.

Enabling Act

Hitler moved to amend the Constitution to allow the government to introduce laws without the Reichstag's approval for four years. This required the support of two-thirds of the Reichstag.

Hitler therefore ensured that most opponents were not there to vote against the measure. With the Communist deputies already in jail, Hitler just needed the support of the Centre Party to achieve the two-thirds needed. This was achieved by a promise to protect the rights of the Catholic Church. When it came to the vote, only the Social Democrats opposed the measure.

Gleichschaltung

Within months, Hitler had eliminated most of the remaining political opposition in Germany as the government implemented a process known as *Gleichschaltung* (co-ordination of all aspects of life to fit in with Nazi ideals).

◆ In April 1933 Jews and political opponents were removed from jobs in the civil service and legal profession. Key positions within Germany's state governments were taken over by Nazis.
◆ In May 1933 all trade unions were outlawed and replaced by a Nazi union, the DAF (German Labour Front).

◆ In July 1933 Germany became a one-party state. However, by this stage there were few other parties to get rid of. The Social Democrats had already been banned, whilst the Centre Party had dissolved itself.

◆ In January 1934 Hitler introduced the *Law for the Reconstruction of the State*. This abolished all of Germany's state governments apart from Prussia's, which was to be run by Herman Göring, a leading Nazi.

Tasks

1. Create a timeline showing the key political developments, 1933–4.

2. Fill in the following table about the Reichstag Fire:

Date	
How Hitler used the fire to his advantage	
What the decree *For the Protection of People and State* allowed the Nazis to do	

3. Fill in the following information about the Enabling Act:

Why Hitler wanted it	How it was passed	What it meant

4. Fill in the missing information in the following table:

	How it was a source of weakness	How it was overcome
Reichstag		
Cabinet		
Trade unions		
State governments		
Other parties		
Individual opponents		

Nazi Consolidation of Power (II) *WHAT YOU NEED TO KNOW*

The year 1934 marks the move towards the final achievement of dictatorship. It is still confusing, as you need to understand <u>why</u> Hitler had to move against his own movement, <u>how</u> he did this and <u>how</u> his actions gained him the support of the army.

Divisions Within

Hitler's position was still under threat; however, now the danger came from the SA, commanded for the last two years by Ernst Röhm. Under his leadership, the organisation had expanded to over two million members (some historians put it as high as 4.5 million).

Röhm believed that Hitler's take-over would be followed by a second revolution in which the power of Germany's economic old guard and the army would be shattered and the SA would become Germany's new army. Röhm now wanted this second revolution to start.

Röhm's plans worried the army, which made clear its displeasure to Hitler. This concerned Hitler for two reasons:

◆ He feared the army. It was the only group that could challenge his power and authority.
◆ He needed the army. Many of its leaders supported his foreign policy aims.

Hitler acted on the night of 30 June 1934, an event that became known as the 'Night of the Long Knives'. Anyone he suspected of threatening his control of the party was eliminated. Key SA leaders, including Röhm, were executed. So too were a number of old political opponents, including General von Schleicher and Gustav von Kahr. In total, nearly 200 people were killed.

Führer

With the SA threat gone, the only remaining obstacle was Hindenburg. He died on 2 August 1934. A day earlier, a new law was passed combining the posts of Chancellor and President and giving all powers to Hitler, who would become Führer and Reich Chancellor.

The army now demonstrated their gratitude to Hitler for the eradication of the SA threat by swearing an oath of personal loyalty to the Führer. From this point on, their fate was inextricably linked to his.

Tasks

1. Create a timeline showing the key political developments in 1934.
2. Fill in the table to explain the Night of the Long Knives:

Reasons	Impact

3. Fill in the missing information in the following table:

	How it was a source of weakness	How it was overcome
SA		
Hindenburg		
Army		

4. Match the solution to the weakness in the following activity to show how each was overcome. Remember that one solution might have helped to overcome more than one weakness.

Weakness	Solution
Reichstag	Night of the Long Knives
Cabinet	Army oath of loyalty
Hindenburg	
Army	Law for the Protection of the People and State
Trade unions	Death
State governments	
Other parties	Enabling Act
SA	1933 election

Hitler in Control *WHAT YOU NEED TO KNOW*

You need to understand three things about Nazi control policies:

1. *Why they wanted to control each aspect;*
2. *What steps they took to ensure control;*
3. *How successful each of these policies was.*

The Nazis sought the creation of a ***volksgemeinschaft*** (people's community). Here, people would know their primary loyalty was to the state and to the Führer. Achieving this meant that all key institutions would come under Nazi control.

To support the Führer a control system was established across the country:

◆ *Reichsleiter* – leading Nazis
◆ *Gauleiter* – provincial leaders
◆ *Kreisleiter* – regional leaders
◆ *Zellenleiter* – cell leaders
◆ *Blockleiter* – local leaders.

While this system helped ensure that the Nazi Party was aware of the mood and thoughts of the population, establishing total control would require even greater interference.

Task

1. Create a flow diagram illustrating how the Nazis' system of control operated.

Propaganda *WHAT YOU NEED TO KNOW*

Propaganda was one of the key Nazi methods of control. You should be able to identify the <u>different methods</u> the Nazis used and explain <u>whether or not</u> they worked.

One of the easiest ways of ensuring conformity was by winning the people over to the regime. This was the job of Dr Joseph Göbbels, Minister for Popular Enlightenment and **Propaganda**.

One of the most spectacular propaganda methods the Nazis used were the annual Nuremberg rallies. Light, sound and costume were used to create a mesmeric atmosphere. Other smaller-scale rallies were held throughout the year.

Control of the media was also a key aim. This was achieved in a variety of ways:

◆ Most newspapers were bought up by *Eher Verlag*, the Nazi publishers.
◆ Journalists had to be approved by the Nazis.
◆ The Editors' Law held editors responsible for the content of their newspapers.
◆ Newspapers that printed stories the regime disapproved of were shut down.
◆ Newspaper editors went to a daily Propaganda Ministry briefing to be told what to print.
◆ All radio stations were brought under Nazi control.
◆ People were encouraged to buy cheap radios made by the Reich Radio Company. These could only pick up Nazi broadcasts. By 1939, 70 per cent of households owned one.
◆ Loudspeakers were erected in public places.

The Propaganda Ministry also controlled **censorship**. To this end, it censored cinema, theatre, music and literature, to ensure that they conformed to Nazi ideas. In May 1933, 20,000 books were symbolically burned in Berlin.

It is difficult to decide the extent to which ordinary Germans believed Nazi ideas. It is probably safe to say that Nazi propaganda helped reinforce existing beliefs but was less successful in trying to get people to accept new ideas. Censorship ensured that the quality of much of Germany's culture was damaged. Only in the area of cinema was high-quality work produced, particularly by Leni Riefenstahl.

Tasks

1. Complete the following table:

Area to control	Methods used
Newspapers	
Radio	

2. Create a spider diagram illustrating all of the different propaganda and censorship methods used by the Nazis.
3. Analyse the success of Nazi propaganda using the headings of (i) Successes and (ii) Failures.

Women WHAT YOU NEED TO KNOW

You need to explain <u>what</u> role the Nazis saw women having in Germany, <u>how</u> they went about achieving their aim and <u>how</u> successful they were.

For the Nazis, a woman's role was neatly encapsulated by the 3 Ks – *Kinder, Kirche und Küche* – Children, Church and Cooking. A number of strategies were implemented to achieve this:

1. Some women – particularly those married or in the professions – were forced from the workplace.
2. By giving every newly married couple a loan of 1000 marks, 25 per cent of which was written off for every child born, the *Law for the Encouragement of Marriage* of June 1933 encouraged women to marry and have large families.
3. Women who had large families were awarded the Mother's Cross. They also received additional welfare benefits and were liable for lower rates of tax.
4. Contraception and abortion were made more difficult to obtain.
5. Divorce to end childless marriages was made easier.
6. Unmarried mothers were encouraged to live in homes (*Lebensborn*) where racially pure SS men could impregnate them.

These policies had mixed results. Although the birth rate had increased by 1939, it remained lower than it was during the 'Golden Twenties'. A large number of women kept their jobs because of labour shortages, although the numbers of professional women did go down. The numbers of women in jobs actually went up in the later 1930s as the drive for rearmament and **autarky** took off.

Tasks

1. Create a spider diagram showing the different strategies the Nazis used relating to women.
2. Complete the following table:

Area	Evidence it worked	Evidence it failed
Birth rate		
Women in jobs		

3. Analyse the success of Nazi policies towards women using the headings of (i) Successes and (ii) Failures.

Youth *WHAT YOU NEED TO KNOW*

Be clear about <u>why</u> young people were so important to the Nazis and make sure you can explain <u>what</u> the Nazis did to control them.

The Nazis saw **indoctrination** of the youth as the key to their future control of the country. To this end they set about influencing children inside and outside school.

Inside School

The Nazis:

- dismissed Jewish teachers and those regarded as unreliable
- encouraged teachers to join the NSLB (National Socialist Teachers' League). By 1939, 97 per cent of teachers were members
- Nazified the curriculum to reflect the importance of subjects such as History, Biology, Geography and PE
- prepared boys for life in the military and girls for their role as mothers
- established special schools (*Napolas* and Adolf Hitler Schools) to teach Germany's future leaders. Boys identified as high fliers went to *Ordensburgen* (Castles of Order).

Free Time

The Hitler Youth Movement was established to control the activities of young people outside the classroom. Led by Baldur von Schirach, membership became compulsory for certain ages in 1936 and others in 1939. There were a number of different sections to the movement, which again stressed the particular role of boys and girls in the future of Germany:

Age	Boys' Organisations	Girls' Organisations
6–10	*Pimpfen* (Cubs)	
10–14	*Deutsches Jungvolk* (Young German Folk)	*Jung Mädel* (Young Girls)
14–18	*Hitler Jugend* (Hitler Youth)	*Bund Deutscher Mädel* (League of German Girls)
18–21		*Glaube und Schönheit* (Faith and Beauty)

The Nazis' youth policies had mixed results. Evidence suggests that the quality and breadth of education suffered badly. Nor were all young people enamoured with the Hitler Youth. A significant minority avoided joining the Nazi youth movements and instead established rival groups. The two most notable were the Edelweiss Pirates and the Swing Youth.

Tasks

1. Create a spider diagram illustrating the strategies the Nazis used inside school to ensure control.
2. Create a spider diagram explaining the different parts of the Hitler Youth Movement.
3. Analyse the success of Nazi youth policies using the headings of (i) Successes and (ii) Failures.

2004 Past Paper and Mark Scheme

(b) The lives of many Germans changed when the Nazis came to power in 1933.

    (i) How did the Nazis try to control the lives of young people in Germany between 1933 and 1939?

                                                                                  [4]

(b) Reference should be made to some of the following:

    (i)
- Nazis placed great importance on encouraging loyalty of young people to the Nazis. Membership of Nazi youth movements increased from 100,000 to over seven million in 1939.
- Schools encouraged loyalty to the Nazis. Changes in the curriculum aimed to indoctrinate young people with Nazi beliefs, e.g. anti-Semitism.
- Special schools run by the SS to train future Nazi leaders.
- Evidence of some opposition by young people, e.g. the Edelweiss Pirates and the Swing Youth.

Religion *WHAT YOU NEED TO KNOW*

Control of religions was essential as these beliefs represented a threat to the regime. You need to know <u>how</u> the state dealt with the different Churches and understand <u>what</u> its own religion was all about.

Catholicism

In July 1933 an agreement (**concordat**) was signed with the Catholic Church. The Church agreed not to involve itself in politics in return for being allowed to retain control over its schools and youth groups. Initially this arrangement worked well, but by 1936 most of the terms were being flaunted. In 1937 Pope Pius XI responded by condemning the Nazi regime, whilst German Church leaders such as Bishop Clemens von Galen of Münster spoke out strongly against Nazi policies in areas such as euthanasia of the mentally ill.

Lutheranism

The Lutheran Church was divided in its attitude to Nazism. Pro-Nazi Lutherans were known as the German Christians. They were led by Ludwig Müller, who became the first Reich Bishop in July 1933. In 1934 those Lutherans who disagreed with Nazism set up the Confessional Church. One of their leaders was Pastor Martin Niemöller who was arrested by the Nazis in 1937 and sent to Dachau Concentration Camp.

The Nazis also set up their own Church, the German Faith Movement. This was based more upon pagan beliefs than Christian values, and attracted few members.

Overall, the Nazis were unsuccessful in their aim of destroying religion; however they were able to reduce the influence of the Churches. Although a number of individual clerics spoke out against aspects of the regime, by and large the Churches remained more concerned with ensuring their survival.

Tasks

1. Complete the following table:

	Areas of success	Areas of failure
Catholicism		
Lutheranism		
German Faith Movement		

2. Analyse the overall success of Nazi religious policies using the headings of (i) Successes and (ii) Failures.

Anti-Semitism *WHAT YOU NEED TO KNOW*

Nazi policy towards the Jews is one of the key elements of the GCSE course. You must be able to explain the different stages of the policy. Remember that your course does not require you to write about the Final Solution/Holocaust.

Once in power, Hitler wasted no time in putting his **anti-Semitism** into operation.

April 1933	Boycott of Jewish shops.
April 1933	Jews banned from government jobs.
October 1933	Jews banned from media jobs.
September 1935	Nuremberg Laws. There were two main elements: • Jews deprived of many political and economic rights. • Illegal for Jews and Aryans to marry or engage in sexual relations outside marriage.
1935	Jews banned from joining the army.
1936	Persecution of the Jews eased off during the 1936 Olympic Games, which were held in Berlin.
1937	Jewish businesses confiscated.
1938	Jews had to carry identity cards and have their passports stamped with a J-shaped symbol. Jews forced to use new names: Israel for men, Sarah for women.

November 1938	The murder of a Nazi diplomat by a Jew in Paris on 7 November was the catalyst for a massive outbreak of anti-Jewish persecution. It became known as *Kristallnacht*. More than 400 synagogues and 7,500 shops were destroyed. Ninety-one Jews were killed and, over the following months, 20,000 were sent to concentration camps. The Nazis also fined the Jews one billion marks for the damage caused on *Kristallnacht*. They also had to clean up the streets.
November 1938	Remaining Jewish businesses confiscated or closed down.
1939	Jews encouraged to emigrate from Germany.
1939	Hitler spoke of future annihilation of Jews.

As with many European countries, anti-Semitism was common in Germany before 1933. A combination of support (especially resulting from propaganda), education, ignorance and fear ensured that persecution of the Jews was able to go ahead.

Tasks

1. Create a spider diagram illustrating the key elements of the Nazis' policies towards the Jews.

2. Fill in the following information about *Kristallnacht*:

Reasons	Events	Results

2004 Past Paper and Mark Scheme

(b) The lives of many Germans changed when the Nazis came to power in 1933.

    (ii) How did the Nazis treat Jews in Germany between 1933 and 1939?

                                                                                 [5]

(b) (ii) Reference should be made to some of the following:
- Jews blamed for Versailles and Germany's economic problems.
- Propaganda against the Jews in film, newspapers and posters.
- 1933 boycott of Jewish-owned shops and the sacking of Jews from jobs in the civil service, education and law.
- 1935 Nuremberg Laws; Jews could not be German citizens or marry a German.
- Lost right to vote, go to university or own a shop. In 1938 they had to add Jewish names Sarah and Israel to their names for identification.
- *Kristallnacht*. The destruction of Jewish businesses and synagogues. Ninety-one were killed and 20,000 put in concentration camps.

The Police State *WHAT YOU NEED TO KNOW*

You need to be able to explain:
1. <u>what</u> the police state was
2. <u>how</u> it worked
3. <u>whether or not</u> it was successful.

'Protective Custody'

Just in case anyone remained unpersuaded by Nazism, the security and justice systems also came under state control. The decree *For the Protection of People and State* allowed for opponents to be arrested and placed in 'protective custody' in concentration camps, the first of which was established at Dachau in March 1933. While most early inmates tended to be political prisoners, before long, other groups suffered **internment,** including:

◆ criminals
◆ the 'work shy'
◆ gypsies
◆ homosexuals
◆ the 'anti-social'
◆ Jews.

Between 1933 and 1939, over 200,000 Germans were convicted and imprisoned for political crimes. In the same period, over 160,000 Germans were placed in 'protective custody'.

Security Forces

Following the Night of the Long Knives Heinrich Himmler's SS became the Party's main police force. In conjunction with the Gestapo and SD, the SS eliminated all opposition within Germany. Historians argue that the SS became so powerful that it became a 'state within a state'.

The Gestapo (the secret state police and a branch of the SS) arrested 'enemies of the state'. Also led by Himmler, much of the information it worked on came from ordinary Germans denouncing others. The SD was the intelligence arm of the SS; headed by Himmler's protégé Reinhard Heydrich, it monitored the security of the Reich.

Judiciary

The judicial system also came under state control. The aim was to ensure that the legal system did not protect those that the state wanted to punish. Special People's Courts were established to judge those accused of crimes against the state.

Overall, the police state was very successful. Although individuals might have grumbled about aspects of the Nazi state, there was no real organised opposition to the regime until World War II.

Tasks

1. Create a spider diagram showing the different groups that ended up in concentration camps.

2. Complete the following table:

Group	Leader	Function
SS		
Gestapo		
SD		

3. Analyse the success of the Nazi police state using the headings of (i) Successes and (ii) Failures.

Nazi Economic Policy (I); Unions and Unemployment
WHAT YOU NEED TO KNOW

This is a crucial area for you to get to grips with. Economic collapse had helped Hitler gain power and people expected a lot from him in this area. You need to know what he did to reduce the power of the unions and tackle the high levels of unemployment.

Destroying the Unions

Hitler was afraid that unions could interfere with his plans and so, in May 1933, they were banned and strikes were declared illegal. Unions were replaced by the German Labour Front (DAF – *Deutsche Arbeitsfront*) led by Dr Robert Ley. Within two years, all workers were members. While the DAF was meant to represent the workers in discussions with the employees, it tended to side with employers, and workers found their freedom restricted and their working hours increased. On a positive note, wages improved, and prices and rents were strictly controlled by the state.

Free Time

The Nazis were also keen to ensure that their workers were happy outside the workplace. Therefore, Strength Through Joy (KDF – *Kraft Durch Freude*) was established in November 1933 to improve workers' free time. Again led by Dr Ley, the KDF provided cheap holidays and organised a broad range of sporting activities. Workers were also given the chance to pay into a savings scheme to own a car, the *Volkswagen* (people's car). However, no cars had been distributed when the war started in 1939.

Unemployment

One of the most important tasks facing Hitler was the need to reduce unemployment. By the end of 1939, only 300,000 Germans were officially listed as unemployed. This was achieved in a number of ways:

1. The scale of existing public work schemes was increased with the establishment of the National Labour Service (RAD – *Reichsarbeitsdienst*). The RAD built schools, hospitals and motorways. Those involved lived in camps and wore military-style uniforms. While no wages were paid, workers got free meals and pocket money. The RAD became compulsory in 1935.
2. Many people – especially professional women and Jews – were forced from the workplace and their jobs were then given to those who were unemployed. Neither of these groups was then counted as unemployed.
3. The introduction of conscription in 1935 had a significant impact on unemployment levels.
4. As Germany prepared for war, thousands of jobs were created in the armament and associated industries. Likewise, the drive for autarky (economic self-sufficiency) resulted in the creation of new industries focused on creating synthetic replacements for raw materials.

Tasks

1. Fill in the following information about the destruction of the trade unions:

Why it was done	How it was done	What it meant for workers	What it meant for the state

2. Complete the following table:

	DAF	KDF
Purpose		
Leader		
Strategies introduced		
Reasons it was good for workers		
Reasons it was bad for workers		

3. Create a spider diagram illustrating the strategies introduced to lower unemployment.

Nazi Economic Policy (II); Stability and Autarky
WHAT YOU NEED TO KNOW

Economic recovery was also essential for Hitler's foreign policy objectives. You need to know <u>what</u> he did to achieve his objectives and be able to assess <u>how successful</u> he ultimately was.

New Plan

In May 1933, respected economist Dr Hjalmar Schacht became President of the *Reichsbank*. Within a year, he had been appointed Minister of Economics. Schacht's 1934 New Plan oversaw the revitalisation of the German economy by:

◆ drastically reducing welfare spending
◆ imposing limits on imports
◆ implementing a series of trade agreements with countries to ensure that Germany was supplied with vital raw materials in return for German industrial goods
◆ introducing targeted government spending on key industries.

Under Schacht's guidance, the German economy recovered; however, this was not enough to ensure his survival. By 1936 Hitler was pressurising him to increase spending on rearmament. Since Schacht was reluctant to do this, he was increasingly ignored and a year later he had resigned from the government.

Four Year Plan

Despite his total lack of economic expertise, Herman Göring was the man Hitler appointed to prepare the economy for war. In 1936 he introduced the Four Year Plan. Its aim was to ensure that Germany was economically self sufficient during any future conflict.

The Four Year Plan introduced a range of strategies to ensure autarky (economic self-sufficiency):

◆ New factories were constructed.
◆ Import levels were reduced.
◆ Higher targets were set for the production of essential materials such as oil, rubber and steel.
◆ Industries were encouraged to develop *ersatz* – synthetic substitutes for raw materials.

However, by 1939 Germany was still importing over 30 per cent of its raw materials. It had become clear that the only way to make its economy self-sufficient was to seize the resources of other states through military conquest.

Task

1. Complete the following table:

	New Plan	Four Year Plan
Purpose		
Person in charge		
Strategies introduced		
Areas of success		
Areas of failure		

2005 Past Paper and Mark Scheme

(c) Explain how and why the lives of workers in Germany changed between 1933 and 1939.

Use the following to explain your answer:
- Public works and RAD.
- Rearmament and conscription.
- KDF (Strength Through Joy). [12]

(c) Reference should be made to some of the following:

Public works and RAD
- Public work schemes had been set up by the Weimar Government.
- The Nazis expanded and reorganised the National Labour Service or RAD; 80,000 were employed in building motorways.
- From 1935, all 18–25 year olds had to spend six months on RAD work. They were only given pocket money. The RAD scheme was organised along military lines and had strict discipline: workers wore uniforms and did drill like soldiers.
- The public work schemes took millions off the unemployment figures, which fell from six million in January 1933 to one million in January 1938.

Rearmament and conscription
- In 1935 the Nazis introduced conscription. This reduced unemployment by 1.4 million by 1939.
- From 1936 Hitler began a programme of rearmament developed by Göring's Four Year Plan.
- Hundreds of thousands of jobs were created in munitions factories, iron works, coal mines, etc.

KDF (Strength Through Joy)
- The Nazis banned trade unions in 1933. Workers lost the right to negotiate better wages and conditions in the RAD schemes, though they now had secure jobs.
- The KDF scheme was promoted to gain Nazi control of workers' lives.
- The campaign gave workers cheap holidays, concerts, sporting facilities, etc.
- The Nazis also promised workers the Volkswagen, an affordable car for the German worker. In reality, few workers received them.
- The standard of living for most German workers in the 1930s remained quite low.

Section 3 Nazi Policy towards Europe

Nazi Foreign Policy WHAT YOU NEED TO KNOW

You need to know <u>what</u> Hitler wanted to achieve with his foreign policy. You should be clear about his initial policies (1933–5) and <u>how</u> Britain and France responded to them.

Aims

Hitler had three main foreign policy aims:

1. To restore Germany's military strength by removing the military restrictions imposed by the Treaty of Versailles.
2. To unite all those claiming German nationality into the Third Reich (*grossdeutschland*).
3. To create *lebensraum* by acquiring new territory in the East to support the growing German population.

Disarmament

At the 1919 Paris Peace Conference it had been agreed that all countries would disarm. However, Germany was the only country that did so. It was decided that an international conference would be held in 1933 to sort out this problem.

Germany demanded that other powers disarm. When France refused, Hitler withdrew Germany from the World Disarmament Conference and from the League of Nations. At the same time, he balanced what might have been seen as an act of belligerence by signing a Non-Aggression Pact with Poland in January 1934.

Rearmament

Throughout the Weimar years, Germany had been secretly rearming. Hitler continued with this policy, but once he felt secure in power, military expenditure tripled and rearmament speeded up:

1. The navy began to construct new vessels.
2. The air force (**Luftwaffe**) expanded rapidly.
3. Conscription was publicly announced in 1935, although the army had already been increasing in size.

All of these actions broke the terms of the Treaty of Versailles. In response, the leaders of Britain, France and Italy met at Stresa to condemn German infringements of the Treaty. However, within two months this coalition, the so-called Stresa Front, had collapsed as a result of Britain signing a Naval Agreement with Germany. This allowed Germany to build a navy of up to 35 per cent of the size of the British fleet.

This was a massive diplomatic victory for Hitler:

1. The anti-German coalition was broken up.

2. The German navy was only about 10 per cent of the size of the Royal Navy at that time.
3. It was yet another breach of the Treaty of Versailles. The difference this time, however, was that one of the countries that had signed the Treaty was involved in its breach.

There were also other successes for Hitler at this time. The Versailles settlement had provided for a future plebiscite to decide who would control the Saar region. This vote took place in January 1935. Over 90 per cent voted for a return to German rule.

Tasks

1. Create a spider diagram illustrating Hitler's main foreign policy objectives.
2. Create a timeline of developments in foreign policy, 1933–5.
3. Fill in the following table concerning rearmament:

Developments pre-Hitler	
Why Germany withdrew from the World Disarmament Conference	
Rearmament under Hitler, 1933–5	
Steps taken to speed up rearmament	
Allied reaction (Stresa Front)	

4. Analyse the 1935 Anglo-German Naval Agreement using the following headings:

Reasons	Details	Impact

1936 *WHAT YOU NEED TO KNOW*

1936 is a key year in Hitler's foreign policy as he began to flex his military muscles for the first time. Make sure you are aware of <u>what</u> he did and <u>how</u> it impacted on international relations. In particular, be clear about what appeasement was.

The Rhineland

In March 1936, the German army reoccupied the hitherto demilitarised Rhineland. This move was clearly Hitler testing the waters to see how the **Allies** would react. He knew that German forces were still comparatively weak and had ordered them to retreat if challenged.

However, France and Britain took no action, preferring to negotiate a peaceful solution rather than use force to uphold the Treaty of Versailles. This strategy became known as **appeasement,** and until 1939 it allowed Germany to expand with impunity. Neville

Chamberlain (British Prime Minister 1937–40) was a strong supporter of appeasement. His willingness to concede to Hitler's demands only increased Hitler's belief in the Allies' weakness.

Alliances

By the end of 1936, military agreements had been made with:

◆ Italy (the Rome–Berlin Axis)
◆ Japan (the Anti-Comintern Pact).

Hitler had also sent troops to help General Franco's nationalist forces in the Spanish Civil War. Not only was this an attempt to help establish a like-minded system and perhaps secure another ally; it also allowed the *Luftwaffe*, flying as the Condor Legion, to perfect aerial bombing methods that would later be used in World War II.

By 1936 it was clear that Hitler was intending to go to war. In that year, he gave Göring the task of overseeing the creation of a war economy through the Four Year Plan. A year later, as recorded in the Hossbach Memorandum, Hitler secretly told his generals that he envisaged Germany being involved in a major war by the mid 1940s.

Tasks

1. Create a timeline of developments in foreign policy, 1936–7.
2. Analyse the remilitarisation of the Rhineland using the following headings:

Reasons	Results

3. Write a sentence to explain each of the following foreign policy developments in 1936–7:

Development	Explanation
Rome–Berlin Axis	
Anti-Comintern Pact	
Spanish Civil War	
Four Year Plan	
Hossbach Memorandum	

Anschluss WHAT YOU NEED TO KNOW

Do you know <u>why</u> Hitler wanted an Anschluss, <u>how</u> he went about achieving it and <u>what</u> the Allies did in response? These are key elements in any analysis of Nazi foreign policy in 1938.

Failure

In July 1934, Austrian Nazis attempted to take power in their country; but Hitler failed to support them, for two reasons:

1. Germany was still militarily weak.
2. Italy had threatened to send troops to protect Austria if necessary.

By 1938 things were very different; Italy was now Germany's closest ally, and Hitler felt that he was strong enough to attempt an *Anschluss*.

Success

In early 1938, Hitler forced Austrian Chancellor Schuschnigg into appointing Nazis to his government. Schuschnigg was so concerned about the impact of Hitler's increased influence that he announced there would be a plebiscite over Austria's future. He hoped that Austrians would vote against an *Anschluss*.

Hitler was outraged and demanded that the plebiscite be cancelled and that Schuschnigg resign. The Austrian Chancellor agreed and was replaced by Austrian Nazi, Artur Seyss-Inquart. He immediately requested the entry of German troops into his country. This happened on 12 March 1938. A subsequent referendum on the *Anschluss* resulted in 99 per cent approval for the action. Again, the Allies protested but did nothing else, thus encouraging further expansion.

Task

1. Analyse the *Anschluss* using the following headings:

Reasons	Events	Results

Czechoslovakia *WHAT YOU NEED TO KNOW*

Czechoslovakia is probably the most complicated part of Hitler's foreign policy. Try to break it down into parts and try to understand exactly <u>what</u> happened, <u>why</u> it happened and <u>what</u> the implications for European peace were. Again, be aware that appeasement plays a key part here.

The Sudeten Crisis

Hitler's next target was Czechoslovakia. He started by launching a propaganda campaign against the country, arguing that the three million Germans living in the industrially developed Sudetenland region were being mistreated.

British Prime Minister Neville Chamberlain was so concerned about the prospect of war that he flew to meet Hitler at Berchtesgaden in September 1938. Hitler demanded that Germany be given all parts of the Sudetenland which were over 50 per cent German. Britain and France persuaded Czechoslovakia to accept these demands.

Hitler now upped the pressure by demanding that the Sudetenland be handed over to him by 1 October. However, the Czechs refused and negotiations broke down. With war seemingly inevitable, another meeting was held at Munich. Hitler announced in advance of this meeting that this would be his last territorial demand in Europe.

Munich

The Munich Conference marked the high point (or low point) of appeasement. Apart from Chamberlain and Hitler, the conference was attended by the leaders of France (Daladier) and Italy (Mussolini). Amazingly however, Czechoslovakia's leader, (Beneš), was not invited, and Czechoslovakia's main ally, the Soviet Union, was excluded.

There were two main terms:

1. Germany would gain the Sudetenland.
2. Hitler agreed to the holding of plebiscites in mixed areas of Czechoslovakia and promised to respect the independence of what remained of Czechoslovakia.

Broken Promises

Hitler still wasn't satisfied. In March 1939, he forced the Czechs to hand over the provinces of Bohemia and Moravia. For the first time, Hitler had taken over non-German territory. Days later, Slovakia – all that remained of Czechoslovakia – came under German protection.

Britain and France's immediate response was to issue a protest against Germany's actions. Not surprisingly, Hitler ignored their disapproval and continued in the same vein by successfully demanding Memel from Lithuania.

Tasks

1. Create a timeline illustrating the key developments with regard to Czechoslovakia, *before* the Munich Conference.

2. Analyse the Munich Conference using the following headings:

Why it took place	
Who was there	
Who was not there	
What was decided	
What did Hitler promise	

3. Create a time line illustrating the key developments *after* the Munich Conference.

The Road to War *WHAT YOU NEED TO KNOW*

This last section covers the final countdown to war and its development up to 1941. The highlight is the Nazi–Soviet Pact so make sure you understand what it was all about.

Nazi–Soviet Pact

Finally realising that Hitler could not be trusted, Britain and France drew up a guarantee of security for Poland on 31 March 1939. Hitler believed that it would be difficult for them to protect Poland and chose to ignore their actions. Preparations for an invasion were stepped up. Perhaps to ensure that he had some allies, a full military alliance, the Pact of Steel, was signed with Italy in May.

Tied in with *lebensraum,* was Hitler's desire for the destruction of communist Russia. Other powers were amazed, therefore, when Nazi Germany and Soviet Russia, two ideological enemies, signed the Nazi–Soviet Pact on 23 August 1939.

As well as agreeing not to attack each other for ten years, the pact contained a secret agreement to divide Poland up between themselves. This left Germany free to attack Poland without taking the risk of having to face Russian troops.

As far as Hitler was concerned, the Nazi–Soviet Pact cancelled out any threat of Britain and France defending Poland. On 1 September 1939 therefore, Germany launched its long-expected attack upon Poland. This, in turn, led to Britain and France declaring war upon Germany two days later.

Blitzkrieg

Nothing much happened in the war for the next few months; then in April 1940 German troops rapidly occupied Denmark and Norway. Control of the latter provided Germany with Atlantic bases and a guaranteed supply of iron ore. In May, Germany invaded Holland, Belgium and France. The use of *Blitzkrieg* allowed the German army to defeat the Dutch, Belgian and French forces within six weeks. The remaining British and French troops were pushed back to Dunkirk from where they were rescued.

Although Britain now stood alone against Germany, she refused to surrender and, as a result of the *Luftwaffe's* failure to win the Battle of Britain, Operation Sea Lion (the invasion of Britain) had to be postponed.

Yet Russia remained Hitler's real goal, and on 22 June 1941, Germany launched Operation Barbarossa, the invasion of the USSR.

Tasks

1. Create a timeline showing the key developments in foreign policy, 1939–41.

2. Write a sentence to explain each of the following foreign policy developments in 1939:

Development	Explanation
Allied security guarantee for Poland	
Pact of Steel	

3. Analyse the Nazi–Soviet Pact using the following headings:

Reasons	Terms	Results

4. Create a spider diagram showing all of the countries invaded by Germany, 1939–41.

KNOWLEDGE TESTS

Knowledge Test I (Pages 13–19)

1 Why did anti-war protests emerge in Germany during World War I?

2 What did the Kaiser hope to achieve by handing power over to a civilian government?

3 Where did a naval revolt break out in November 1918?

4 On which date did the Kaiser abdicate?

5 Who replaced the Kaiser as Germany's leader?

6 What happened on 11 November 1918?

7 Why were ordinary Germans so shocked by this event?

8 Which group attempted to overthrow the new government in January 1919?

9 Name the two leaders of this group.

10 Who were the Free Corps?

11 What was strange about the government using the Free Corps to defeat the *putsch*?

12 Name one other city that experienced a communist rebellion in 1919.

13 Why did Germany become known as the Weimar Republic?

14 Why was proportional representation a potential weakness for the Weimar Republic?

15 What did Article 48 of the Weimar Constitution state?

16 How could Article 48 undermine democracy in Germany?

17 Name one country Germany lost land to as a result of the Treaty of Versailles.

18 What size of an army did the Treaty of Versailles allow Germany?

19 What did Article 231 of the Treaty of Versailles state?

20 What impact did the Treaty have on people's attitudes to the Weimar Republic?

Knowledge Test II (Pages 19–24)

1 Who was the leader of the Free Corps rising of March 1920?
2 What led the Free Corps to rebel at this time?
3 Why was Ebert forced to ask the workers to go on strike?
4 How did the government reward the Ruhr workers who had defeated the Kapp *Putsch* but remained on strike?
5 What was the name of the Weimar Foreign Minister who was assassinated in 1922?
6 What was the total amount of reparations that Germany was to pay?
7 Why did France and Belgium invade the Ruhr in January 1923?
8 How did the government react to this invasion?
9 Name THREE ways in which the government's policy made the economic situation worse.
10 What is hyperinflation?
11 Name TWO groups that were particularly affected by the hyperinflation crisis.
12 Name THREE steps that Stresemann took to solve Germany's economic problems.
13 What did the Dawes Plan do?
14 What did the Young Plan reduce the reparations total to?
15 What was agreed in the Locarno Treaty?
16 Which international organisation did Germany join in 1926?

Knowledge Test III (Pages 24–7)

1 Name one piece of evidence that suggests that Germany was politically stable, 1924–9.
2 Name one piece of evidence that suggests that Germany was NOT politically stable, 1924–9.
3 Name one piece of evidence that suggests that Germany was economically stable, 1924–9.
4 Name one piece of evidence that suggests that Germany was NOT economically stable, 1924–9.
5 In which country was Hitler born?
6 What did Hitler do after the war was over?
7 What was the name of the political party that Hitler joined in 1919?
8 What name was given to the policy proposals of this party?
9 Name ONE of the party's policies.
10 What was the SA?
11 In which month of 1923 did Hitler attempt to stage a rebellion?
12 Which World War I hero supported his plans?
13 Why did the rebellion fail?
14 How did Hitler turn his trial to his advantage?
15 How long did Hitler spend in prison?
16 What was the name of the book that Hitler wrote while in prison?
17 What significant tactical change did Hitler make while in prison?
18 What was *Führerprinzip*?
19 Name ONE new organisation set up by the Nazi Party at this time.
20 How did the Nazis perform in the 1928 General Election?

Knowledge Test IV (Pages 28–31)

1. Which TWO disasters befell the Weimar Republic in October 1929?
2. Name TWO economic results of the events of October 1929.
3. Who resigned as Chancellor in March 1930?
4. Why did this Chancellor resign?
5. Who became Germany's new Chancellor?
6. How many seats did the Nazis win in the September 1930 general election?
7. What nickname was this Chancellor given?
8. Give TWO reasons why he was given this name.
9. How many Germans were unemployed by late 1932?
10. Why were there two presidential elections in 1932?
11. Who became Chancellor in May 1932?
12. How many seats did the Nazis win in the July 1932 general election?
13. Why was there another general election in November 1932?
14. How many seats did the Nazis win in the November 1932 general election?
15. Why was Kurt von Schleicher appointed Chancellor in December 1932?
16. How long did von Schleicher serve as Chancellor?
17. On which date was Hitler appointed Chancellor?

Knowledge Test V (Pages 33–5)

1. Name THREE limitations that Hitler faced in his quest for dictatorship.
2. How did the Nazis take advantage of the Reichstag fire?
3. What special law was passed in the aftermath of the Reichstag fire?
4. How many seats did the Nazis win in the March 1933 general election?
5. Name TWO things that the Nazis did to ensure the passage of the Enabling Act.
6. What did the Enabling Act allow Hitler to do?
7. What was *Gleichschaltung*?
8. What happened to Germany's trade unions in May 1933?
9. In which month of 1933 did Germany become a one party state?
10. What did the *Law for the Reconstruction of the State* do?
11. Who was the leader of the SA?
12. Give TWO reasons why Hitler now regarded the SA as a threat.
13. Give ONE reason why Hitler was concerned by the army's reaction to the SA threat.
14. What event took place on 30 June 1934?
15. Who died on 2 August 1934?
16. How did the army demonstrate its loyalty to Hitler?

Knowledge Test VI (Pages 36–9)

1 What was the *volksgemeinschaft*?
2 Who was in charge of propaganda for the Nazis?
3 Where were the main Nazi rallies held each year?
4 Name THREE ways in which the Nazis tried to ensure control of the media.
5 Give ONE way in which the Nazis censored books.
6 What were the 3Ks?
7 Name TWO ways in which Nazis tried to ensure their aims for women were fulfilled.
8 Why did the number of women in work increase in the later 1930s?
9 Name THREE ways in which the Nazis tried to control education.
10 What were *Ordensburgen*?
11 Who was Baldur von Schirach?
12 Name TWO parts of the Hitler Youth movement.
13 Name TWO anti-Nazi youth groups.

Knowledge Test VII (Pages 40–6)

1 What was the 1933 Concordat?
2 Name ONE Catholic leader who spoke out against Nazi policies.
3 Who were the German Christians?
4 Who was the leader of the German Christians?
5 What was the Confessional Church?
6 Name a key leader of the Confessional Church.
7 What was the German Faith Movement?
8 What is anti-Semitism?
9 Name ONE point of the 1935 Nuremberg Laws.
10 Why did persecution of the Jews ease off in 1936?
11 What was *Kristallnacht*?
12 Name TWO groups that ended up in concentration camps.
13 Which Nazi organisation became known as a 'state within a state'?
14 What was the KDF?
15 Name TWO steps taken to reduce unemployment in Germany after 1933.
16 Who was Hjalmar Schacht?
17 What was the Four Year Plan?
18 Did the Four Year Plan work?

Knowledge Test VIII (Pages 48–54)

1 Name TWO of Hitler's main foreign policy aims.
2 Name ONE international organisation that Germany left in 1933.
3 With which European country did Germany sign a Non-aggression Pact in 1934?
4 In which year was conscription publicly announced?
5 What was the Stresa Front?
6 Why did the Stresa Front collapse?
7 Which area of Germany did its army march into in 1936?
8 What was appeasement?
9 Name ONE alliance that Germany agreed in 1936.
10 What was the Condor Legion?
11 What did Hitler reveal in the Hossbach Memorandum?
12 How had the relationship between Italy and Germany changed between 1934 and 1938?
13 Who invited the German army into Austria in 1938?
14 Why did Hitler want the Sudetenland?
15 Which TWO countries were not represented at the Munich Conference?
16 With which country did Germany sign a Pact in August 1939?
17 What was Operation Sea Lion?
18 Which country did Germany invade in June 1941?

Chapter 3 PEACE, WAR AND NEUTRALITY: BRITAIN, NORTHERN IRELAND AND IRELAND AND THE SECOND WORLD WAR c1932–49

Section 1 Anglo-Irish Relationships before World War II

Ireland before 1932 *WHAT YOU NEED TO KNOW*

Before looking at political developments in Ireland after 1932, you should gain a little contextual knowledge of how and why Ireland was partitioned and what impact partition had.

Partition

Before 1920 Ireland was a single unit ruled by Britain. In that year it was **partitioned** by the Government of Ireland Act. Two new states were set up, Northern Ireland and Southern Ireland.

Northern Ireland

The Government of Ireland Act delighted **unionists**. They lost no time in holding elections for the new parliament and their leader, Sir James Craig (from 1927, Lord Craigavon), became the first Prime Minister of Northern Ireland.

Many **nationalists** resented the new state, leaving unionists convinced that they wanted to destroy it. These fears led to the introduction of a range of repressive measures:

◆ The establishment of the mainly Protestant Ulster Special Constabulary. It had a part-time section called the B Specials who were particularly feared by Catholics.
◆ The introduction of the Special Powers Act in 1922. This allowed the Government to arrest and detain people without trial.
◆ The abolition of **proportional representation** to ensure increased control over nationalist councils, and the **gerrymandering** of electoral boundaries.

Irish Free State

The terms of the Government of Ireland Act were unacceptable to Irish **Republicans**, and in 1921 the Anglo-Irish Treaty superseded it. This established the Irish Free State as a **dominion** of the British Commonwealth.

Irish Republicans were divided by this measure, particularly:

1. the inclusion of an Oath of Allegiance to the British monarch
2. the confirmation of the partitioning of Ireland.

The divisions were so serious that a **civil war** was fought between 1922 and 1923. Eventually, the pro-Treaty side was victorious and, under the leadership of Cumann na nGaedheal, the Free State set about increasing its independence from Britain. This culminated in the passage of the 1931 Statute of Westminster, which stated that dominions were independent countries that could leave the Commonwealth without Britain's permission.

During this period Éamon de Valera led the anti-Treaty side. In 1926 he established a new party, Fianna Fáil. It entered the Dáil (Irish Parliament) in 1927 and within a year had become the official opposition party.

The Free State under de Valera *WHAT YOU NEED TO KNOW*

Once in power, de Valera moved rapidly to put some distance between the Free State and Britain. You will be expected to be able to explain the <u>different steps</u> that he took and <u>how</u> they impacted on Anglo-Irish relations.

Cementing Independence

Following a **General Election** in March 1932, Fianna Fáil, with Labour Party support, became the Free State's government. Bit by bit, de Valera began to remove the Free State's remaining links with Britain.

1. In November 1932, London recalled **Governor General** James MacNeill because Fianna Fáil ministers were engaged in a policy of snubbing him. He was replaced by Fianna Fáil politician Domhnall O'Buachalla, who was given the title of *an seanasca*. O'Buachalla's powers were limited; he never lived in the Governor General's official residence in Phoenix Park and he undertook no official duties.
2. In May 1933, the Government passed the Removal of the Oath Act, eliminating the Oath of Allegiance that all members of the Dáil had to swear to the King.
3. In May 1933, the Free State Constitution was changed to prevent citizens appealing Irish Court verdicts to the British **Privy Council**. London challenged these actions before the Privy Council in 1935, however it ruled that the Statute of Westminster permitted de Valera's actions.
4. De Valera used the December 1936 **abdication crisis** to pass the External Relations Act. With this, the King's role within the Free State came to a end, although in theory the Free State continued to recognise the monarch as Head of the Commonwealth. As a result, the office of Governor General also ceased to exist.

Tasks

1. Create a timeline illustrating the key developments in the Irish Free State's relationship with the British Commonwealth, 1932–6.
2. Using the following headings, write a summary of the steps de Valera took to redefine the Irish Free State's relationship with the British Commonwealth:

Area	De Valera's actions
Governor General	
Oath of Allegiance	
Privy Council	
Abdication crisis	

The Economic War *WHAT YOU NEED TO KNOW*

This period can be quite confusing. Make sure you understand <u>what</u> caused the Economic War, <u>what</u> form it took, <u>how</u> it was ended and <u>what</u> impact it had on relations within the British Isles.

Land Annuities

From 1870, the British Government loaned Irish tenants money to buy their own land. Each year, the farmers had paid back a part of the loan. The payments were known as land annuities. Between 1922 and 1932 the money was collected by the Irish Government and passed on to London.

Many Irish farmers resented making these payments and, following his election, de Valera stopped them. He argued that:

1. Ireland was experiencing the effects of an economic depression
2. as Northern Ireland's land annuities had been abolished, so too should the Free State's.

The Economic War

Britain responded to de Valera's actions by imposing duties of 20 per cent on Free State imports. The Irish Government, in turn, imposed taxes on imports from the United Kingdom. The stand off continued for six years, although in 1935 both sides took a step back from the brink by agreeing a trade-increasing Coal–Cattle Pact.

The Economic War had two main effects:

1. **The Irish economy**
   Irish farmers probably suffered most with a 35 per cent reduction in cattle exports (from 1929 levels), resulting in massive overproduction of beef. This was despite the Government trying to encourage them to explore new markets by increasing production

of crops such as wheat and sugar beet. As a result, living standards fell even though taxes were raised to compensate farmers. At the same time, small-scale farmers did benefit from the reduction of the annuity payments, now made to the Dublin Government.

While the industrial sector wasn't quite as badly hit, it wasn't a massive success either. Although de Valera hoped that increasing the price of British goods would encourage the development of Irish industries, this failed to happen. On the other hand, the lack of coal did result in a period of growth for the peat industry.

2. **Relations between Britain, Northern Ireland and Ireland**
   The Economic War led to a deterioration in Dublin's relations with both London and Belfast. Economically, it had a much greater impact on the Northern Irish economy, than on the British economy.

Tasks

1. Analyse the beginning of the Economic War using the following headings:

Land annuities before 1922	
Land annuities 1922–32	
Why de Valera withheld payment	
British response	
Irish response	
De Valera's hopes for Irish industry	

2. Examine the impact of the Economic War by writing a sentence on each of the following areas:

Impact on the Irish economy	Impact on relations between Britain, Northern Ireland and Ireland

The 1937 Constitution *WHAT YOU NEED TO KNOW*

Constitutions can be a little confusing! You must be able to explain <u>what</u> the key articles of Bunreacht na hÉireann were, and <u>how</u> London and Belfast reacted to them.

Bunreacht na hÉireann

In 1937 de Valera introduced a new constitution, *Bunreacht na hÉireann*. It included three significant changes:

1. The name of the state would become Éire.
2. The leader of the Government was to be the *Taoiseach*.

3. A new (largely ceremonial) Head of State would be elected every seven years. That person would be given the title of President.

The Constitution recognised the special position of the Catholic Church, although 'freedom of conscience and the free profession and practice of religion' was granted to other faiths. Article II claimed political jurisdiction over the whole island. However, Article III added that until the end of partition, Éire's laws would only apply to the 26 counties that made up Éire.

The Constitution made no mention of the King, yet Éire remained as a member of the Commonwealth. De Valera believed that keeping this link with Britain might make it easier to end partition. However, with the changes introduced in 1937, Éire became a **republic** in all but name. In 1938, Douglas Hyde, a renowned Gaelic scholar, was elected President.

Reactions

Unsure whether Éire remained in the Commonwealth or not, London treated the changes introduced as insignificant. Unionists were not so calm. *Bunreacht na hÉireann* reinforced their fears and suspicions of their neighbours, and strengthened their determination to remain within the United Kingdom.

The unionist Government – located at **Stormont** since 1932 – strongly criticised *Bunreacht na hÉireann*. In particular, it condemned Article II with its territorial claim over Northern Ireland, and denounced the special recognition given to the Catholic Church and the Irish language. Lord Craigavon used the opportunity to call a snap general election in 1938, resulting in an increased majority.

Despite the inclusion of Articles II and III, it could be argued that by removing almost all links with Britain, *Bunreacht na hÉireann* had reinforced partition, making re-unification unlikely. As a result, Northern nationalists continued to feel isolated.

Tasks

1. Create a spider diagram illustrating the three key constitutional changes made.

2. Analyse the terms of *Bunreacht na hÉireann* using the following headings:

Catholic Church	
Other faiths	
Northern Ireland	
King	
Commonwealth	

3. How did the following groups react to *Bunreacht na hÉireann*?

British Government	Northern Irish Government	Northern Nationalists

Britain and the Threat of War *WHAT YOU NEED TO KNOW*

Appeasement is a key element of British foreign policy in the 1930s. You should be able to explain <u>what</u> it was, <u>why</u> it was adopted and <u>why</u> it was finally abandoned.

Tensions in Europe

The emergence of **Fascism** and **Nazism** in the 1930s, with their expansionist foreign policies, endangered Britain's security. Similarly, the growth of **Communism** created problems. Tensions in Europe grew further following Italy's attack on Abyssinia and as a result of the Spanish Civil War (1936–9).

Britain had a number of options as the risk of war grew:

1. **Neutrality**
   A neutral Britain would not get involved in any war. While there were many who supported such a policy, Britain also had to consider the protection of her empire.

2. **Rearmament**
   While rearmament would be costly, a 1935 report on Britain's military readiness made grim reading. Faced with Germany's military expansion, Britain was forced to increase defence spending.

3. **Appeasement**
   In the end Britain adopted **appeasement** as its main policy for the following reasons:

   ◆ People still remembered the horrors of the Great War and were keen that the government did not commit itself to another conflict.
   ◆ Britain's economy was still recovering from the impact of the Great War and the Great Depression, and was not in a position to bear the costs of rapid rearmament.
   ◆ Many politicians – particularly British Prime Minister Neville Chamberlain – viewed Hitler as a reasonable man with reasonable demands who could be dealt with by reasonable policies.

Impact

Appeasement allowed Britain to begin rearmament albeit at a slower rate. In particular, improvements were made to the size of the Royal Navy and the RAF, which also benefited from the development of modern fighter and bomber aircraft and of **radar**.

However, Hitler took advantage of appeasement. While there was no great opposition to the remilitarisation of the Rhineland, the 1938 *Anschluss* with Austria and particularly Hitler's treatment of Czechoslovakia in 1938 and 1939 discredited appeasement, and led Britain and France to offer military guarantees to Poland in an effort to prevent a German attack. Confident that the August 1939 Nazi–Soviet Pact neutralised Russia as an opponent, Hitler ignored the Anglo-French guarantees and invaded Poland in September 1939. When Britain's ultimatum to withdraw was ignored, war was declared on 3 September 1939.

Tasks

1. Create a spider diagram illustrating Britain's options in the face of the threat of war.

2. Complete the following table:

Reasons appeasement introduced	Reasons appeasement ended	How appeasement benefited Britain

---

2003 Past Paper and Mark Scheme

(a) (i) Give **two** reasons why Britain followed a policy of appeasement in the 1930s.

[2]

(ii) Give **two** examples of how Britain prepared for war before 1939.

[2]

(a) (i) Any **two** of the following:
- War too expensive.
- Memories of World War I.
- Felt that Hitler's demands were reasonable.
- Fear of Communism.
- Role of Chamberlain.

Any other valid point [1] for each correct answer.

(ii) Any **two** of the following:
- Increased the size of the airforce/reorganised RAF;
- Rearmament;
- Tried diplomacy with Éire;
- Civilian defence;
- Shelters;
- Radar;
- Evacuation;
- Plans for rationing.

Any other valid point [1] for each correct answer.

The Anglo-Irish Agreements *WHAT YOU NEED TO KNOW*

You must be able to explain the reasons <u>why</u> Britain and Éire decided to end their differences and understand the <u>different reactions</u> to their decision.

The British Prime Minister Neville Chamberlain decided that the growing tensions in Europe made it sensible to improve Anglo-Irish relations. This would mean:

1. ending the Economic War
2. resolving the issue of the Treaty Ports.

Chamberlain recognised the strategic value of the ports, but he decided that returning them would help end the Economic War and would result in Éire's assistance if war broke out.

For his part, de Valera was keen to get the ports back. He wanted to safeguard Éire's neutrality and believed that British control of the Treaty Ports undermined Éire's claims to such neutrality.

On 25 April 1938, British and Irish delegations signed three separate agreements that ended the Economic War and returned the Treaty Ports to Éire. Éire agreed to pay Britain £10 million to resolve the annuities question, while all duties imposed by both countries during the Economic War were removed.

While the Agreements received a favourable response from most people, the return of the Treaty Ports was sharply criticised by Winston Churchill. Unionists were particularly concerned about the improvement in Anglo-Irish relations, fearing that it might result in the ending of partition.

Tasks

1. Complete the following table summarising the different attitudes to the issue of the Treaty Ports:

Chamberlain's attitude	De Valera's attitude

2. Analyse the Anglo-Irish Agreements under the following headings:

Date	
Key terms	
Majority response	
Churchill's response	
Unionist response	

2004 Past Paper and Mark Scheme

(b) (i) How did the Economic War affect the Irish economy in the 1930s?

[4]

    (ii) How did the Anglo-Irish Agreement of 1938 end the Economic War?

[5]

(b) (i) For the top marks, reference should be made to some of the following:
- Big drop in beef and dairy exports to Great Britain – led to overproduction at home and consequent slaughter of cattle; increased taxes to compensate farmers.
- Decline in rural living standards.
- Effects on industry not as severe as agriculture. Attempt made to build up Irish domestic industry – not very successful; raw materials from Great Britain were too expensive, especially coal and iron products.
- The peat industry benefited because of the scarcity and cost of British coal.

Any other valid point.

    (ii) For the top marks, reference should be made to some of the following:
- Specific terms of the Anglo-Irish Agreement of 1938.
- Removal of all special taxes on British and Irish goods sold in each jurisdiction. Trade war ended.
- Britain transferred the Treaty Ports to Éire.
- Éire paid £10 million as a final payment for land annuities.

Any other valid point.

Developments in Northern Ireland, 1938–9 *WHAT YOU NEED TO KNOW*

You need to be able to explain the <u>reasons</u>, <u>details</u> and <u>outcomes</u> of these important issues to the examiner.

IRA

In January 1939, the IRA ordered Britain to leave Northern Ireland within four days. When nothing happened, they launched a bombing campaign in Britain. London introduced emergency measures – including internment – to deal with the IRA threats. The Dublin Government did likewise.

Conscription

In April 1939, the British Government announced the introduction of **conscription**. However, the fear of a negative nationalist reaction led to Northern Ireland being exempted. An irate Craigavon demanded that the decision be reversed. This, in turn, annoyed nationalists, and the North's Catholic bishops issued a statement opposing his request. De Valera also voiced his concerns.

In May 1939, Chamberlain met Craigavon to explain that the reason for the decision not to introduce conscription was Northern Ireland's 'special difficulties'.

To compensate for the refusal to extend conscription, Northern Ireland was awarded over £6 million in defence contracts. Particularly involved were the Short and Harland aircraft factory and the Harland and Wolff shipyard. While this resulted in a fall of over 30,000 in the number of unemployed during 1939, it also meant that Belfast could be a target for enemy bombers.

Tasks

1. Analyse the 1939 IRA bombing campaign by completing the following table:

Reasons	British reaction	Irish reaction

2. Create a spider diagram on conscription showing (1) those in favour and (2) those against.

3. Complete the following table about defence production:

Amount awarded to Northern Ireland companies	
Companies that benefited	
Impact on unemployment	
Dangers for Belfast	

Section 2 Experience of and Response to War

Ready for War? *WHAT YOU NEED TO KNOW*

This is an important section and can be quite confusing. Make sure that you are able to identify both positive and negative aspects of Northern Ireland's preparations for war.

Complacency?

Northern Ireland was not ready for war when it started in September 1939. The administration continued to believe that the country was beyond the range of enemy aircraft.

Even after the war had begun, the Government was slow to act. It was not until well into 1941 that the majority of the province was covered by radar, and steps had been taken to establish a number of anti-aircraft batteries. Even then, some feared that enemy planes could still approach Northern Ireland without being picked up, while others suggested that far too few anti-aircraft defences were in place.

By June 1940, German forces had reached the English Channel and the possibility of air attack increased. While a significant reorganisation of the RAF within Northern Ireland took place in response, it remained too poorly resourced to be able to protect the province properly.

Nor did the reaction in Northern Ireland compare well to the comprehensive evacuation and air raid protection schemes implemented in Britain. No effort was made to launch evacuation plans for Belfast until July 1940. Even then, only a small proportion of Belfast's children were evacuated. Meanwhile, nearly a year after the declaration of war, only 15 per cent of Belfast households entitled to an Anderson air raid shelter had taken delivery of one.

MacDermott's Reforms

Things did begin to improve a little when, in June 1940, John MacDermott was appointed Minister of Public Security. He organised:

◆ the rapid erection of public air-raid shelters
◆ the reinforcement of the emergency services
◆ efforts to evacuate children from Belfast.

However, it was too little too late and when, in April and May 1941, the *Luftwaffe* bombed Belfast, the city still only had a limited number of anti-aircraft guns, insufficient air cover and public shelters capable of housing no more than a quarter of the city's population.

Public responses to the dangers of air attack were almost as inept as those of the Government. Although steps were taken to introduce Civil Defence measures, the service remained voluntary, unlike that in Britain. To make matters worse, ARP (Air Raid Precautions) wardens were not taken seriously as they went about their duties and blackouts were routinely ignored. In spite of constant warnings, the majority of people did not carry gas masks until after the Belfast Blitz.

Task

1. Examine Northern Ireland's preparation for war, 1939–41:

Year	Positive developments	Areas of concern
1939		
1940		
1941		

The Battle of Britain *WHAT YOU NEED TO KNOW*

The Battle of Britain was a crucial early moment in the war. Make sure that you are clear about <u>why</u> it happened in the first place and <u>why</u> the RAF was ultimately victorious.

Preparing for War

By the end of June 1940, Britain stood alone against Germany. However, her army was incapable of defending Britain from a German invasion. Steps were swiftly taken to address this situation:

1. Factories worked multiple shifts to produce aircraft, tanks and heavy weapons.
2. Over 500,000 rifles were ordered from the USA.
3. The Local Defence Volunteers (Home Guard) was established in May 1940. By August 1941 there were over a million members.

However, the RAF was in a stronger position due to the programme of improvements that had been ongoing since 1935. Radar provided early warning of enemy aircraft, while the RAF itself was reorganised to reflect different defence priorities.

Preparations for war included the development of a civil defence plan. This included:

◆ mass evacuation plans for women and children
◆ the distribution of gas masks
◆ the provision of 400,000 Anderson air raid shelters
◆ the establishment of the ARP force to enforce blackout regulations.

Battle for the Skies

In July 1940, Britain – now led by Winston Churchill – rejected Hitler's offer of peace terms. Hitler responded by ordering the implementation of Operation Sea Lion, the invasion of Britain. However, before this could be implemented, the RAF would have to be destroyed, as its control of the skies would prevent a sea invasion.

On 12 August 1940 the *Luftwaffe* launched its attack on the RAF. It is likely that if these attacks had continued, the RAF would have been worn down. However, on 7 September the *Luftwaffe* switched tactics and started to bomb London. This was in response to recent RAF raids on Berlin. The raids continued for months and were extended to include other British cities.

While the nightly Blitz caused widespread destruction, the change of tactics allowed the RAF to regroup and obtain new aircraft. The bombing of London delayed Operation Sea Lion and, with the RAF undefeated, it was cancelled in October 1940.

Tasks

1. Create a spider diagram illustrating how Britain prepared for war.
2. Analyse the Battle of Britain using the following headings:

Reasons why the Battle of Britain began	Different stages	Outcome

The Belfast Blitz *WHAT YOU NEED TO KNOW*

There are three key aspects of the Belfast Blitz for you to get your head around:
1. *Why it happened;*
2. *Its impact on lives, property and industry;*
3. *Its political impact.*

Targeting Belfast

In 1941, it was Belfast's turn to experience the effects of the Blitz. Belfast was targeted because:

1. Germany was aware of the key role that a number of Belfast's industries were playing in the war effort
2. Northern Ireland was playing an important strategic role in the war.

For these reasons, the *Luftwaffe* visited Belfast four times during April and May 1941.

◆ Close to 1000 civilians were killed.
◆ Over 56,000 homes were damaged or destroyed, leaving in excess of 100,000 people homeless.
◆ Belfast's industrial infrastructure suffered extensive damage. It took six months for industrial production to recover.

Leadership Changes

The Blitz highlighted the poor effort that Stormont was making of the Northern Ireland war effort. Upon his death in 1940, Craigavon had been replaced as Prime Minister by his Finance Minister, J M Andrews. Unfortunately he was not up to the demands of the job, yet obstinately refused to compensate for his own shortcomings by bringing in younger, more able ministers.

Despite its loyalty to the Unionist Party, the unionist voting public was not beyond sending a warning shot across the Party's bows. In 1942, two safe seats were sacrificed in by-elections. By 1943, the situation had deteriorated further. Faced with the threatened resignation of his two most able ministers, Basil Brooke and John MacDermott, Andrews resigned. The new Prime Minister was Basil Brooke.

Tasks

1. Analyse the Belfast Blitz using the headings of (i) Reasons and (ii) Results.
2. Complete the following summary table:

	Craigavon	Andrews	Brooke
Dates in office			
Reasons for appointment			
Reasons for leaving office			

2004 Past Paper and Mark Scheme

(c) From 1939 to 1945 Northern Ireland was at war with Germany.

(i) Why did Germany target Belfast during World War II?

[6]

(ii) Why did the German bombing raids cause so much loss of life and damage in Belfast during World War II?

[6]

(c) (i) For the top marks, reference should be made to some of the following:
   • Important aircraft factory and munitions factories.
   • Shipbuilding.
   • Strategic value.
   • Part of the UK and a legitimate target.
   Any other valid point.

(ii) For the top marks, reference should be made to some of the following:
   • Lack of preparation by the Stormont Government. Complacent attitude as it did not believe Belfast would be a target.
   • Lack of adequate defences — only 22 anti-aircraft guns, few barrage balloons.
   • Measures to protect the civilian populations were inadequate and were not enforced, e.g. shelters for only a quarter of the people in Belfast; civilians were not evacuated although air raids were expected by the Government.
   • Germans carried out sustained attacks on central, north and east Belfast near densely populated areas. Over 5000 of the houses in Belfast were damaged and nearly 1000 people were killed.
   • Harland and Wolff shipyard was very badly damaged.
   Any other valid point.

Northern Ireland's War Effort (I) Strategic *WHAT YOU NEED TO KNOW*

There are several different aspects to Northern Ireland's strategic role in the War. Make sure that you can comment in detail on the <u>different roles</u> that she played.

Conscription Again

In the aftermath of the Belfast Blitz, the British Labour Minister, Ernest Bevin, again raised the possibility of conscription. Again, most nationalists opposed the move, seeing this as Britain's war, not theirs. Aside from de Valera condemning the proposal, thousands of nationalists took to the streets of Belfast in protest, supported by the local Catholic hierarchy and nationalist politicians.

Some unionists also believed that conscription was more trouble than it was worth. The RUC Inspector General informed the Government of his fear that serious public disorder could result from any attempt to introduce conscription. Once more London announced that conscription would not be extended to the North.

Military Service

Instead of being conscripted, men and women volunteered to join the armed services. It is estimated that close to 40,000 people from Northern Ireland served in the war. Just over 10 per cent died. In excess of 43,000 Éire citizens fought for the **Allies**. However, the legacy of Anglo-Irish relations meant that their contribution was not recognised at home.

Northern Ireland's experience of the Home Guard differed markedly from Britain's. The fear of republican infiltration if the force was created through open enrolment meant that the Northern Ireland Home Guard was based around the B Specials. Unlike Britain, the force came under the control of the RUC rather than the army.

As was the intention, Catholic membership of the movement was limited and the Home Guard came to be seen as little more than a sectarian force. Although the British Government expressed some unease at this situation, they did nothing about it.

Much of the focus of the Home Guard was on counteracting the IRA threat. Pro-German sentiments were evident in some republican circles and the Government introduced internment to deal with IRA suspects.

Strategic Significance

Northern Ireland's location ensured that it played a key role in the war. Naval bases, particularly Derry/Londonderry, provided services for those vessels involved in the Battle of the Atlantic and acted as bases for vessels keeping sea-lanes open. Furthermore, air bases at locations such as Ballykelly, Eglinton, Nutts Corner, Long Kesh and Castle Archdale provided much needed cover for convoys. Northern Ireland was also used as a base for preparations for D Day.

Tasks

1. Analyse the 1941 conscription crisis using the headings of (i) Those in favour and (ii) Those against.

2. Assess the Northern Ireland Home Guard under the following headings:

How recruited (compared with Britain)	
Why recruited in this way	
How commanded (compared with Britain)	
Catholic attitude to and involvement in the Home Guard	

3. Create a spider diagram illustrating Northern Ireland's strategic importance to the war effort.

Northern Ireland's War Effort (II) Economic *WHAT YOU NEED TO KNOW*

There are two key aspects of Northern Ireland's economic war effort that you need to understand. Make sure that, where necessary, you can comment on areas of success and areas of failure.

Agriculture

The best-performing section of the Northern Ireland wartime economy was agriculture, and Ulster's farmers prospered. With increasing demand in Britain for food, the amount of land under tillage increased by 60 per cent. Likewise, the numbers of cattle and poultry increased significantly. The latter were responsible for providing Britain with 20 per cent of its egg consumption. Along with eggs, Britain received sheep, cattle and dairy produce.

There were several reasons for this impressive performance, christened the 'Dig for Victory':

1. Continued availability of fertilisers.
2. The more than one-hundred-fold increase in tractor numbers.

However, a significant amount of credit belongs to the Minister for Agriculture, Basil Brooke. His success in this area played no small part in his selection, in May 1943, as Prime Minister.

Rationing

The war resulted in the introduction of rationing to discourage waste and encourage self-reliance. Although shortages did not bite as quickly as they did in Britain, by 1941 goods such as fresh meat and dairy produce became much more difficult to source, particularly in towns. Fuel shortages had a massive impact on the use of cars. For some, particularly those close to the border, smuggling alleviated the shortages, for others, the solution was recourse to the black market.

Industry

The fortunes of Northern Ireland's industrial economy were not quite as impressive. On the one hand, industrial production started to improve, and unemployment fell from a high of 70,000 in 1941 to just 10,000 three years later. At the same time, wages and the standard of living improved. On the other hand, productivity was hit by:

◆ bad management
◆ questionable working practices
◆ a series of strikes (even though they were meant to be illegal).

That said, the industrial economy did play some part in the drive for victory. By the time the war ended, much of the industrial unrest had dissipated and production figures had begun an upward climb. A variety of Northern Ireland firms produced a significant number of tanks, ships, aircraft and munitions.

Tasks

1. Examine Northern Ireland's agricultural performance using the following headings:

Examples of improvement	
Reasons for improvement	

2. Examine Northern Ireland's industrial performance using the following headings:

	Evidence	Reasons
Success		
Failure		

War and the Free State (I) Military Preparations

WHAT YOU NEED TO KNOW

You must be clear about how Dublin responded to the start of the Second World War. In particular you need to be able to explain what military changes were introduced.

Neutrality

The day after Britain declared war on Germany, de Valera announced Éire's neutrality. He correctly assumed that the population would support neutrality as another way of reinforcing Éire's independence and protecting the country from the ravages of war.

The Government responded by passing the Emergency Powers Act, which allowed it extensive powers. Censorship was introduced and strictly enforced.

Military Preparations

Despite neutrality, there remained the possibility that Ireland might be invaded by Germany as a precursor to an invasion of Britain. This scenario also held out the possibility of the British army moving back into Ireland to secure its vulnerable western flanks.

Well aware of the limitations in its armed forces, the Government extended the defence forces until there were over 40,000 in the army, 250,000 reserves in the Local Defence Volunteers (albeit largely unarmed), an extended navy and a newly established air force.

Yet the Irish armed forces remained poorly equipped. It is unlikely that they would have been able to prevent any invasion. Therefore, de Valera agreed to invite the British army in to help repel any German invasion.

The IRA

De Valera moved against the IRA as a result of its rather inept efforts to make common cause with the Third Reich against the British. Using the Offences against the State Act, the Government introduced internment without trial against suspected IRA members. Six IRA members were hanged and when a further three went on hunger strike they were allowed to die. De Valera's stance was supported by the vast majority of the population. In the event, the Government's onslaught left the IRA broken.

Tasks

1. Analyse the Dublin Government's response to the threat of invasion, under the following headings:

Emergency Powers Act	
Defence forces	
Invitation to Britain for assistance	

2. Examine de Valera's actions against the IRA, using the following headings:

Actions	Reasons	Outcomes

War and the Free State (II) Assessing Neutrality

WHAT YOU NEED TO KNOW

You must be clear about <u>how</u> neutrality operated in practice and <u>how</u> it impacted on Anglo-Irish relations.

Joining the War?

Britain made two main attempts to woo Ireland to her side after Winston Churchill became Prime Minister in May 1940.

1. In June 1940, London proposed the reunification of Ireland if Éire joined the Allies. However, de Valera rejected the offer on the strength of the negative impact it would have on Éire's independence.
2. Following the Japanese attack on Pearl Harbor, Churchill telegrammed de Valera. His offer of 'Now or never "A nation once again"', was understood by de Valera to refer to the possibility of Irish unity if he joined the Allies, but again he declined.

Totally Neutral?

Frequently, however, Dublin's actions indicated that their neutrality was biased in favour of the Allies.

◆ German pilots who bailed out over Éire were imprisoned, while Allied airmen were allowed to cross the border into Northern Ireland.
◆ During the Belfast Blitz, de Valera sent fire engines to help.
◆ Allied airmen were permitted to fly over Irish territory through their use of the 'Donegal Air Corridor'.
◆ In the final months of the war, de Valera allowed the RAF to establish a number of secret radar bases on Irish territory.

On occasion, though, de Valera also went to quite extraordinary lengths in his efforts to display even-handedness. He outraged Allied opinion when, in April 1945, he visited the German Ambassador to express sympathy over Hitler's death. Earlier the same month, however, he had carried out a similar visit to the American Ministry as a mark of respect to the late US President, Franklin Delano Roosevelt.

Whose Credit?

It is important to consider the real reasons for Éire's ability to remain neutral.

1. Éire benefited from the sympathetic attitude of the representatives of the British and German Governments in Dublin, and their recommendations to their respective governments not to do anything that would compromise that neutrality.
2. If the Allies had found it strategically necessary to invade the South, they would have done so. That they did not was due mainly to the significant strategic role that Northern Ireland played during the conflict.

This possibility was revealed in a speech delivered by Churchill on the war's conclusion, when he condemned de Valera's role in the conflict whilst praising the part played by Northern Ireland. De Valera used his response to score a few palpable hits of his own. He asked Churchill if he could not 'find in his heart the generosity to acknowledge that there is a small nation that stood alone, not for one year or two, but for several hundred years against aggression?'

Tasks

1. Create a spider diagram showing how Éire's neutrality was biased towards the Allies.

2. What part did the following play in Éire's successful maintenance of neutrality during the war?

German and British Ambassadors	
Northern Ireland	

The Impact of the 'Emergency' *WHAT YOU NEED TO KNOW*

Make sure that you can explain to the examiners <u>how</u> life in Ireland changed as a result of the war.

The war – or 'Emergency' as it was called – impacted on Ireland in a number of ways:

◆ Poor *Luftwaffe* navigation resulted in Dublin being bombed several times.

◆ The Ministry of Supplies was set up under Sean Lemass to ensure that Ireland was not left totally without essential materials. He established the Irish Shipping Company to carry supplies previously brought by British ships. However, factories still had to close because they could not get hold of sufficient raw materials or industrial machinery. Particularly in short supply were petrol and coal. As a result of the lack of coal, the consumption of turf increased many times over.

◆ Ireland benefited from a food surplus. However, the lack of available fertilisers damaged the productivity even if more land was under tillage. In addition, other imports such as tea and sugar had to be rationed. Attempts were made to increase wheat production to support the production of bread. Unfortunately, the Irish climate was not best suited to this crop and so rationing had to be introduced.

◆ Other goods to be rationed included butter, while fruit and chocolate became unavailable. As a result, smuggling increased. At the same time, the availability of most meat and dairy produce, in addition to the potato, meant that most people were able to survive without having to tighten their belts too much.

◆ The closure of factories had an impact on employment levels and many Irish people began to seek their fortunes in Britain. It is estimated that between 1939 and 1945 about 200,000 Irish people crossed the Irish Sea.

◆ Despite the general support for neutrality, the harsh economic situation meant that Fianna Fáil still lost ten seats in the 1943 General Election. Within a year, all but one of these seats had been regained in another election. The explanation for a second poll following on so quickly from the first was the Allies' decision to quarantine Ireland in advance of D Day. The reason for this was de Valera's refusal of an American request to shut down the German and Japanese Ministries in Dublin to prevent leaks of the Allied invasion plans.

Task

1. Assess the impact of the war on Éire using the following headings:

Industry	
Agriculture	
Rationing	
Employment and emigration	
Support for Fianna Fáil	

Section 3 Post-War Relationships

The Welfare State (I) Great Britain *WHAT YOU NEED TO KNOW*

*The introduction of the **Welfare State** was a major turning point in the history of the United Kingdom. You need to be able to explain <u>why</u> it was introduced and <u>how</u> it worked.*

Labour in Power

In May 1945 World War II ended in Europe; two months later the Labour Party, led by Clement Attlee, won the British General Election.

The new Government faced a difficult situation:

◆ Britain was close to bankruptcy.
◆ Poverty was widespread.
◆ Most manufactured goods were being exported to pay for food imports.
◆ There were acute shortages of coal, whilst bread and potatoes had to be rationed for the first time in 1946.

As a result, the immediate post-war period was known as the 'age of austerity'.

Reforms

Labour believed that the state should control Britain's key industries. This policy of **nationalisation** was implemented as follows:

1947	coalmines
1947	electricity
1948	railways
1949	iron
1949	steel

As they had promised, the Labour Government responded to the existence of slums and bomb damage by implementing a massive house-building policy. On average, 170,000 houses were erected each year between 1947 and 1950.

The National Health Service came into operation in July 1948. Despite initial opposition from those concerned about the costs in terms of increased taxation and from doctors fearing the impact on their independence and private income, the NHS was a major – if costly – success and greatly benefited public health in Britain.

Tasks

1. Create a spider diagram illustrating the problems that the new Labour Government faced.

2. Complete the following table to explain the implementation of Labour's key policies:

Nationalisation	
Housing	
NHS	

The Welfare State (II) Northern Ireland *WHAT YOU NEED TO KNOW*

The Welfare State also impacted on Northern Ireland. You need to be able to explain the <u>initial fears</u> expressed, <u>what</u> was reformed and <u>how</u> well it worked.

Reforms in Northern Ireland

Many in Northern Ireland were worried about what Labour's policies might mean for Northern Ireland. Unionist business leaders feared the implications of nationalisation. Meanwhile, apart from suspicions of socialism, the Government feared the loss of power to a centralising government and wondered how it was to finance the introduction of similar reforms.

It needn't have worried; the Labour Government demonstrated its gratitude for Northern Ireland's contribution to the war effort by subsidising the introduction of the Welfare State. In 1948 the NHS came into operation and the following year saw improvements to family allowance, national assistance, health service (including campaigns against TB and polio) and non-contributing pensions. However, the reforms did make Stormont more financially dependent on Westminster.

The impact of the war had worsened an already serious housing shortage in Northern Ireland. In 1944 it was estimated that 37 per cent of homes were unfit for purpose and over 100,000 new homes were required. In 1945 the Northern Ireland Housing Trust was established to oversee their construction. This massive undertaking took two decades to complete and even then discrepancies in the manner of allocation meant that not all benefited equally.

Radical changes were also introduced to the education sector by the 1947 Education Act. For the first time, all children over 11 were guaranteed free secondary education up to the age of 15. Those who passed the 11+ examination had the opportunity to attend grammar schools. New schools were constructed to cope with the increased numbers in education, while funding for the voluntary sector increased to 65 per cent.

Tasks

1. Analyse the background to the introduction of the Welfare State, using the following headings:

Economic concerns	
Political concerns	

2. Analyse the reforms introduced in Northern Ireland under the following headings:

NHS	Housing	Education

2003 Past Paper and Mark Scheme

(a) (i) Give **two** examples of problems faced by the working classes before the introduction of the Welfare State.

[2]

(ii) Give **two** reasons why there was some opposition to the introduction of the Welfare State.

[2]

(a) (i) Any **two** of the following:
- Poor housing.
- Poor healthcare.
- Healthcare costs/doctors' fees.

Any other valid point [1] for each correct answer.

(ii) Any **two** of the following:
- Doctors worried about impact on them.
- Seen as too much state control.
- Wealthier worried about higher taxation to pay for the service.

Any other valid point [1] for each correct answer

Éire: Post-War Problems *WHAT YOU NEED TO KNOW*

The first change of government in sixteen years was a major development in Éire. Make sure that you can explain <u>why</u> this happened and identify the <u>different groups</u> in the new administration. Be clear as well about the new government's <u>policy initiatives</u>.

Depression

Éire found itself isolated economically after 1945. Dissatisfaction with neutrality meant that it would not receive economic priority from London. The outcome was a severe economic depression:

◆ Unemployment shot up.
◆ Building materials became almost unobtainable meaning that houses could not be built.
◆ Britain withheld coal imports.
◆ Éire experienced a harsh winter and severe fuel shortages in 1947.
◆ Rationing remained in force and was extended to include bread from the start of 1947.
◆ Emigration rates remained high.

In contrast to the situation in the North, state benefits (unemployment, family allowance) were almost non-existent and there was no Welfare State to look after people. Instead, individuals had to invest in private medical care. The result was increased unpopularity for the Fianna Fáil Government, and it lost the 1948 General Election.

The Inter-Party Government

As a result of Fianna Fáil's defeat, a **coalition** government took power in Éire. Known as the Inter-Party Government, this administration was made up of a range of political parties:

◆ Fine Gael was the largest of the parties. It was set up in 1933 as a union of a number of parties including Cumann na nGaedheal. It was led by General Richard Mulcahy.
◆ Two different and antagonistic Labour parties.
◆ Farmers were represented by Clann na Talmhan.
◆ Clann na Poblachta was a republican and socialist party. It was led by Seán MacBride who had been Chief of Staff of the IRA from 1936 to 1938.
◆ The Government also had the support of twelve independent **TDs**.

As leader of the largest party, Mulcahy should have become *Taoiseach*. However, he was unacceptable to MacBride because of his involvement in the Irish Civil War. For this reason, senior Fine Gael politician John A Costello was appointed as *Taoiseach*.

Reforms

Under Costello, Éire's economy started to recover with the Government introducing polices to create a modern industrial economy. The Finance Ministry set up state bodies such as the Industrial Development Authority (IDA) in 1949, to start regenerating Éire's economy. The new Government also started a programme to build new houses, about 12,000 annually by 1950. The signing of a trade agreement with Britain in 1948 improved profit margins for Irish agricultural exports.

Tasks

1. Create a spider diagram to illustrate the post-war problems in Irish society and in the Irish economy.
2. Create a spider diagram to explain the different groups involved in the Inter-Party Government.
3. List the steps that the new Government took to try to improve the Irish economy.

Éire Becomes a Republic *WHAT YOU NEED TO KNOW*

The Declaration of the Republic was a key event in modern Irish history. It is important that you can explain <u>why</u> it happened, <u>how</u> different groups reacted to it and <u>what</u> impact it had on partition.

Reasons

The members of the Inter-Party Government – particularly Clann na Poblachta – felt that the 1937 Constitution had left Éire's relationship with Britain in a confused state. Therefore, in November 1948 the Republic of Ireland Bill was introduced into the Dáil. It came into effect on Easter Monday 1949.

Reactions

As Éire was the first country to leave the Commonwealth, there was concern about how Britain would react. However, Australia and Canada supported Éire, stating that the Declaration of the Republic should not impede the development of friendly relations with the Commonwealth.

Due to their close economic links, Britain decided not to regard Éire fully as a foreign state but rather as a neighbour with a special relationship. This meant that:

◆ passports were not needed for travel between the two countries
◆ working permits were not required for Irish workers in the UK
◆ citizens of both nations had voting rights in each other's elections.

Northern nationalists unsuccessfully demanded seats in the Dáil so that their views could be heard. Many of them felt abandoned by Dublin and objected to the claim that the Dublin Government represented all of Ireland.

Fearing – correctly – that Dublin would make a determined effort to end partition, unionists pledged their defiance to the Declaration of the Republic. They rejected Dublin's offers of guarantees to unionists if they joined the new Republic.

Instead, the unionist Government used the border issue as the justification for calling a General Election for February 1949. Brooke urged unionists to use their vote against the threat to their links with Britain. The election became known as the 'Chapel Gate Election'. This was because the money to allow a high number of nationalist candidates – representing the Anti-Partition League – to stand was raised through collections outside churches in the South.

The outcome – after a bitter campaign marred by sectarian violence – was an increased share of votes and seats for both unionists and nationalists. Brooke used this increased support as justification for demanding a British guarantee of Northern Ireland's future within the United Kingdom.

The Ireland Act

Westminster's response was the Ireland Act of June 1949. It stated that 'In no event will Northern Ireland … cease to be part of … the United Kingdom without the consent of the parliament of Northern Ireland'. Effectively, the Stormont Government had been handed a **veto** over their political future. Unionists were delighted.

Dublin and the North's nationalists, on the other hand, were outraged and strongly expressed their displeasure with the Act. However, nothing was changed; Attlee felt that as Dublin had not consulted him about the Declaration of the Republic, he was free to give whatever guarantees he wanted to the North.

Tasks

1. Analyse reactions to the Declaration of the Republic under the following headings of: (i) Commonwealth reaction; (ii) British reaction; (iii) Unionist reaction and (iv) Nationalist reaction.
2. Examine the 1949 Ireland Act under the following headings:

Reasons	Terms	Reactions

2004 Past Paper and Mark Scheme

(c) In 1949 Ireland was declared a republic and the Ireland Act was passed by Britain.

   (ii) Explain how these two acts changed the relationship between Britain and the new Republic of Ireland.

      [6]

   (ii) Explain the response of nationalists and unionists in Northern Ireland to these changes.

      [6]

(c) (i) For the top marks, reference should be made to some of the following:
- Éire introduced the Declaration of the Republic, 1949 – terms and constitutional changes.
- Great Britain passed the Ireland Act 1949 – terms and constitutional changes;
- Britain did not react in a hostile way. Equal rights granted to Irish citizens in Britain; Irish workers in Great Britain would not need work permits; passports were not needed for travel between Great Britain and Ireland; voting rights in each other's elections.
- favoured trading status given to Ireland.
- Northern Ireland's constitutional status was guaranteed in the Ireland Act. Only the Stormont parliament could change it.

Any other valid point.

   (ii) For the top marks, reference should be made to some of the following:
- Unionists saw the Declaration of the Republic as a threat, accompanied as it was by a new drive to end partition.
- Unionist Prime Minister Brooke called an election to allow Northern Irish people to show their support for union.
- Nationalists demanded the right to sit in the Dáil so that the North would be represented – this was refused. Northern nationalists felt abandoned and resented the Declaration of the Republic for the 26 counties.
- Éire politicians agreed to a collection to help finance anti-partition candidates in the election (Chapel Gate Election – name given by *Belfast Telegraph*).
- Unionists annoyed by Éire's attempt to interfere in Northern Ireland's affairs – many bitter sectarian clashes during the election campaign.

Any other valid point.

KNOWLEDGE TESTS

Knowledge Test I (Pages 60–4)

1 What was the name of the Governor General recalled by the British Government in November 1932?

2 What title was given to the man who replaced the recalled Governor General?

3 In what year did de Valera's Government pass the Removal of the Oath Act?

4 Which crisis in the British political system did de Valera take advantage of to pass the External Relations Act?

5 What were land annuities?

6 What happened to the land annuities collected between 1922 and 1932?

7 Give ONE reason used by de Valera to justify withholding the land annuities.

8 What amount of import duties did Westminster impose on all goods imported from the Free State?

9 How did the Dublin Government respond to this action?

10 What evidence is there that Anglo-Irish relations began to improve in 1935?

11 Name ONE way in which the Economic War impacted on the Irish Free State's economy.

12 Which fuel source increased in popularity during the Economic War?

13 In what year did de Valera introduce a new Constitution?

14 What was the official Irish name of the new Constitution?

15 Name ONE key change introduced by the new Constitution.

16 What did Article II of the new Constitution state?

17 Why did de Valera retain a link with Britain in the 1937 Constitution?

18 Who became the first President of Éire?

19 How did Westminster respond to the new Irish Constitution?

20 What action did the Belfast Government take in response to the passage of the new Constitution?

Knowledge Test II (Pages 65–9)

1 What THREE options did Britain have in the face of the threat of another European war?
2 Give THREE reasons for the adoption of appeasement.
3 German actions against which TWO countries finally persuaded Britain and France to abandon appeasement?
4 Why did Hitler ignore the Anglo-French guarantees given to Poland?
5 Why did Chamberlain want to improve Anglo-Irish relations in 1938?
6 Why was de Valera keen to obtain the return of the Treaty Ports?
7 How much did Éire pay to resolve the land annuities issue?
8 Why did Churchill oppose the return of the Treaty Ports?
9 Why were Unionists so concerned by the Anglo-Irish Agreements of 1938?
10 Why did the IRA launch a bombing campaign in Britain in 1939?
11 How did the London and Dublin Governments respond to this campaign?
12 Why did London decide not to introduce conscription to Northern Ireland in 1939?
13 How much money was Northern Ireland awarded in defence contracts in 1939?
14 Name TWO companies that benefited from these contracts.

Knowledge Test III (Pages 70–2)

1 Why was the Northern Ireland Government so slow to prepare for war?
2 How long did it take the Government to improve radar coverage and anti-aircraft defences?
3 Why did the possibility of air raids on Northern Ireland increase after June 1940?
4 In June 1940 who was appointed to head the newly created Ministry of Public Security?
5 Name TWO improvements that this minister made.
6 When did the Belfast Blitz happen?
7 Name TWO ways in which Belfast's defences were still limited when the Blitz happened.
8 Name TWO ways in which ordinary people ignored the dangers posed by air raids.
9 Name THREE steps that Britain took in 1940 to protect herself against German invasion.
10 What was Operation Sea Lion?
11 Why did the *Luftwaffe* need to defeat the RAF?
12 When did the Battle of Britain begin?
13 How did the *Luftwaffe* change tactics in September 1940?
14 Why did the *Luftwaffe* change tactics in September 1940?
15 How did the *Luftwaffe's* change of tactics help the RAF?

Knowledge Test IV (Pages 72–6)

1 Give TWO reasons why the *Luftwaffe* attacked Belfast.

2 How many people were killed as a result of the Belfast Blitz?

3 How many houses were destroyed by the *Luftwaffe* attacks?

4 For how long was production at the shipyard and aircraft factories disrupted by the Belfast Blitz?

5 Who was Prime Minister of Northern Ireland from 1940 to 1943?

6 How did voters express their dissatisfaction with the unionist Government in 1942?

7 Who became Northern Ireland's new Prime Minister in 1943?

8 Which British Minister again raised the issue of introducing conscription in Northern Ireland?

9 Why did London decide for a second time not to introduce conscription into Northern Ireland?

10 Roughly, how many people from the island of Ireland served with the Allies during World War II?

11 Name TWO ways in which Northern Ireland's Home Guard differed from that in the rest of Britain.

12 Name TWO ways in which Northern Ireland was able to play a strategic role in the fighting World War II.

13 Give TWO reasons why Northern Ireland's agriculture sector performed so well in World War II.

14 Which types of goods were rationed in Northern Ireland?

15 By how much did unemployment fall in Northern Ireland between 1941 and 1944?

16 Give TWO reasons for poor industrial productivity in Northern Ireland during the war years.

Knowledge Test V (Pages 76–80)

1 How soon after the start of the war did Éire declare its neutrality?

2 What was the attitude of the majority of Irish citizens to the declaration of neutrality?

3 What law did the Dáil pass to enable it to deal with the dangers caused by the start of the war?

4 Name THREE ways in which the Irish armed forces were improved at this time.

5 What did de Valera agree to do if the German army invaded Éire?

6 How many attempts did Churchill make to get de Valera to join the Allies in the war?

7 Name FOUR ways in which Éire's neutrality favoured the Allies.

8 How many members of the IRA were hanged by the Dublin Government during the war?

9 What action, undertaken by de Valera in April 1945, outraged Allied opinion?

10 List SIX ways in which the war impacted upon life in Éire.

Knowledge Test VI (Pages 81–6)

1 Who became British Prime Minister in 1945?
2 Name TWO problems facing this new government.
3 What was nationalisation?
4 Give TWO reasons why some doctors opposed the introduction of the National Health Service.
5 Give TWO reasons why the introduction of the Welfare State into Northern Ireland was viewed with apprehension.
6 Why did the London Government subsidise the introduction of the Welfare State into Northern Ireland?
7 Which organisation was set up to oversee the introduction of housing improvements into Northern Ireland?
8 What did the 1947 Education Act do?
9 Give TWO pieces of evidence to indicate that Éire was experiencing economic hardship post-1945.
10 Name TWO of the parties that made up the Inter-Party Government that won the 1948 general election.
11 Name ONE economic improvement introduced by the Inter-Party Government.
12 On what date was Éire declared a republic?
13 What right did Northern Ireland nationalists demand in the aftermath of the Declaration of the Republic?
14 By what name was the 1949 Northern Ireland General Election known?
15 What was the main term of the 1949 Ireland Act?

Chapter 4

CHANGING
RELATIONSHIPS: BRITAIN,
NORTHERN IRELAND AND
IRELAND c1965–85

Section 1 Northern Ireland in the 1960s

Northern Ireland before 1963 *WHAT YOU NEED TO KNOW*

This is background information and will not be asked about directly in the exam. However, you should be aware of these facts, particularly those that help explain the problems that emerged in Northern Ireland in the 1960s.

Northern Ireland was established by the 1920 Government of Ireland Act, which partitioned Ireland. The population reacted differently to the Act:

◆ **Unionists** – mostly Protestants – were delighted. Northern Ireland's substantial Protestant majority guaranteed their control of the Government.
◆ **Nationalists** – mostly Catholics – were upset. They wanted to be part of the rest of Ireland.

Violence and Discrimination

As a result, most unionists felt that nationalists could not be trusted and in this atmosphere of distrust the number of **sectarian** killings rocketed. The Government responded by establishing the Ulster Special Constabulary (populated mainly by former members of the **UVF**) and passing the Special Powers Act (1922). This allowed them to arrest and detain suspects without holding a trial.

Other political responses to the seeming threat of nationalism included:

◆ the abolition of **proportional representation** for local elections. This meant that fewer nationalists would be elected to councils
◆ the redrawing of local council boundaries to ensure unionist control even where there was a nationalist majority. This was known as **gerrymandering**
◆ allowing only those who paid **rates** to vote in local elections. For every £10 paid in rates one vote was given, up to a maximum of seven. This usually resulted in extra votes for the wealthy – who tended to be Protestant – and no votes for the poor – who were mostly, but not wholly, Catholic.

Discrimination was also practised against Catholics in other ways:

◆ Catholics were given fewer houses than Protestants by the unionist-controlled councils, as ownership of a house gave a vote in local elections.
◆ The quality of much Catholic housing was inferior.
◆ Catholics were less likely to have a job than Protestants.

Developments up to 1963

By and large, this situation remained unchanged until the 1960s. Northern Ireland played a valuable part in the Allied war effort 1939–45, and in the late 1940s the **Welfare State** was introduced to improve living conditions.

However, relations with the South (the **Republic** of Ireland since 1949) remained tense, particularly as Articles II and III of the South's 1937 **Constitution** laid claim to the whole of the island. Furthermore, between 1956 and 1962, an IRA campaign in opposition to the border reinforced the Government's view that nationalists were untrustworthy. This was despite the fact that the campaign failed due to a lack of nationalist support.

A New Premier *WHAT YOU NEED TO KNOW*

The appointment of Terence O'Neill is a significant moment in this course. You must be able to explain <u>why</u> he wanted to improve the economy, <u>how</u> he tried to do this and <u>what</u> the results of his policies were.

In March 1963 Captain Terence O'Neill replaced the hard-line Lord Brookeborough as Prime Minister of Northern Ireland. Right from the start, O'Neill's leadership was undermined, as most of the Unionist Party's (OUP) MPs had wanted Brian Faulkner to get the job. However, at that time, the OUP leader was decided by a group of senior party members, not by election.

Economic Improvement

O'Neill wanted to modernise the outdated and failing economy. A number of key measures were introduced:

◆ £900 million of investment to update existing industries and attract new ones.
◆ Road and rail network modernised.
◆ Co-operation with the Dublin-based Irish Trades Union Congress (ITUC), whose support was important for economic development.
◆ Economic Council established under Brian Faulkner.
◆ Ministry of Development set up to drive economic revival.
◆ The establishment of a new city called Craigavon.
◆ The development of a new university in Coleraine.

Success and Failure

These policies had a positive impact:

◆ A number of multinational firms (Michelin, DuPont, Goodyear, ICI, Grundig) opened factories in Northern Ireland.
◆ A motorway system was begun.
◆ An oil refinery was opened in Belfast.
◆ A new airport was under development.
◆ An agreement regarding the supply of electricity was agreed with Dublin.

In total, over 35,000 new jobs were created during the 1960s, but at the same time over 20,000 were lost in the ailing traditional industries such as linen manufacture.

This was not the only bad economic news:

◆ Between 1963 and 1969 money had to be given to shipbuilders Harland and Wolff to keep it afloat.
◆ Unemployment averaged between 7 and 8 per cent.
◆ Several companies refused government grants to open factories west of the River Bann, seeing the area as too remote from their export markets.

Tasks

1. Create a spider diagram illustrating the economic measures introduced by O'Neill's government.
2. Analyse O'Neill's economic policies using the headings of (i) Successes and (ii) Failures.

O'Neill's Political Policies WHAT YOU NEED TO KNOW

This is another crucial area. It is essential that you are able to explain why O'Neill wanted to improve relations with the Republic and within Northern Ireland, and what steps he took to achieve this.

O'Neill realised that Northern Ireland also needed social and political modernisation and improvements in her relationship with the South.

The Hand of Friendship: Dublin

In January 1965, O'Neill met *Taoiseach* Sean Lemass at Stormont. He paid a return visit to Dublin four weeks later. Both meetings focused on areas of economic co-operation. Northern and Southern ministers also met to discuss issues such as tourism and electrical link-ups. In 1967, O'Neill met with Lemass' successor, Jack Lynch.

The Hand of Friendship: Northern Nationalists

Within Northern Ireland, O'Neill tried to improve relations with the nationalist community by:

◆ visiting Cardinal William Conway, spiritual leader of Ireland's Catholics
◆ offering official condolences on the death of Pope John XXIII
◆ visiting schools and hospitals run by the Catholic Church
◆ increasing the financial support provided for Catholic hospitals and schools.

Task

1. Create a spider diagram illustrating the steps taken by O'Neill to improve relations with Dublin and Northern Ireland's nationalists.

2005 Past Paper and Mark Scheme

(a) (i) Give **two** examples of O'Neill's attempts to improve relations between the two communities in Northern Ireland in the 1960s.

(ii) Give **two** measures taken by O'Neill to improve the Northern Ireland economy in the 1960s.

[4]

(a) (i) Any **two** of the following:
   • O'Neill met Sean Lemass, *Taoiseach* of the Irish Republic in 1965 and Jack Lynch, *Taoiseach* of the Irish Republic in 1967.
   • O'Neill sent condolence on the death of Pope John XXIII in 1963 and met Cardinal Conway.
   • O'Neill visited Catholic schools and hospitals.
   • UVF made illegal in 1966.

(ii) Any **two** of the following:
   • Ministry of Development was set up to organise economic reform.
   • Five economic zones were set up to attract foreign investment and encourage multinational companies to set up in Northern Ireland.
   • 35,000 new jobs created.
   • New city of Craigavon was built.
   • New motorway system to improve communications.
   • New university to be built at Coleraine.
   • Increased links with the Republic of Ireland led to an agreement on the supply of electricity and the promotion of tourism.

Reactions to O'Neill's Policies *WHAT YOU NEED TO KNOW*

Many of the questions in this examination focus on unionist and nationalist reactions to various events. It is essential that you are able to explain <u>who</u> supported O'Neill, <u>who</u> opposed him and <u>why</u> this was the case.

Unionist Reactions

The OUP did well in the 1965 **general election**, suggesting that O'Neill's policies were enjoying broad support amongst unionist voters. However, Brian Faulkner's condemnation of O'Neill's failure to tell his cabinet he was meeting Lemass suggested there were divisions within the Party.

Lemass's visit was also strongly opposed by the **Moderator** of the Free Presbyterian Church, Rev Ian Paisley. He was concerned about the influence of the Catholic Church in the Republic and objected to Articles II and III of the Republic's Constitution, which laid claim to the whole island of Ireland.

Tensions increased in 1966 with the commemorations for the 50th anniversaries of the Easter Rising and the Battle of the Somme, and rioting broke out. Two people were murdered by the re-emerging **UVF**. O'Neill responded by banning the organisation.

As the situation worsened, O'Neill found that support within the OUP was weakening. In September 1966, he revealed a plot by **backbenchers** to get rid of him. There were also growing rumours of opposition within his own cabinet from Deputy Prime Minister, Brian Faulkner and Agriculture Minister, Harry West.

Nationalist Reactions

Initial support was reflected in the decision of the Nationalist Party to take up the role of **official opposition** in Stormont for the first time in its history. However, support was replaced by frustration as the better future that seemed to have been promised failed to appear. This annoyance was particularly felt amongst a new generation of Catholics. There were a number of reasons:

1. The decision to name the new city linking Portadown and Lurgan, Craigavon, after Northern Ireland's first Prime Minister.
2. The suspicion that O'Neill's economic policies favoured the Protestant East at the expense of the Catholic West. As evidence of this, a number of points were made:
   ◆ Most economic development was in Protestant areas.
   ◆ Unemployment was at a higher level west of the Bann.
   ◆ Despite significant cross-community protest, the new university was sited in the mainly Protestant town of Coleraine, rather than in the mainly nationalist Derry/Londonderry, Northern Ireland's second city.
   ◆ No significant attempts were made to increase Catholic membership of various health and education bodies.

Tasks

1. Analyse unionist reactions to O'Neill's policies under the following headings:

Evidence of unionist support	
Evidence of opposition from within the OUP	
Rev Ian Paisley	
UVF	

2. Create a spider diagram illustrating the evidence put forward by nationalists to suggest that O'Neill's reforms were biased against them.

NICRA: Background *WHAT YOU NEED TO KNOW*

As you might expect, NICRA is a common focus of examination questions. You should know __all__ of the key points about its origins, aims and tactics, and about the different reactions to it.

Origins

The Northern Ireland Civil Rights Association (NICRA) was established in early 1967. It was inspired by:

1. The US Civil Rights Movement;
2. The student demonstrations that had taken place in France in the same year.

Set up as a non-sectarian movement and using peaceful tactics, NICRA did not seek to end partition; rather it hoped to end what it saw as a number of serious abuses in the existing political system. In particular it sought to:

◆ achieve one man, one vote
◆ ensure the fair allocation of council houses
◆ end gerrymandering
◆ prevent discrimination in the allocation of government jobs
◆ remove the operation of the Special Powers Act
◆ disband the B Specials
◆ establish a formal complaints procedure against local authorities to report breaches in the above areas.

Support and Opposition

Support for NICRA came from:

◆ a new generation of Catholics, the first to have benefited from the introduction of free education in the late 1940s. They were unhappy with the performance of their own

Nationalist Party, led by Eddie McAteer. Its only policy seemed to be the ending of partition

◆ some Protestants who sympathised with NICRA's demands and believed that making Northern Ireland fairer for all would undermine demands for a united Ireland

◆ communists

◆ academics

◆ trade unionists.

However, NICRA was seen as provocative, and faced suspicion from many unionists:

◆ Some felt that NICRA was a front for the IRA.

◆ Some believed that NICRA was only interested in Catholic rights and would undermine the position of Protestants.

◆ Some thought that NICRA threatened the continued existence of Northern Ireland.

Tasks

1. Analyse NICRA under the following headings:

Date of establishment	
Sources of inspiration	
Intended support base	
Tactics	
Position on border	

2. Create a spider diagram indicating NICRA's aims.

3. Examine attitudes to NICRA and its campaign using the following headings:

	Support	Opposition
Who?		
Why?		

NICRA: Events *WHAT YOU NEED TO KNOW*

Examiners will expect you to be able to write about NICRA's early marches, their impact and the five-point reform programme.

Marches

The first NICRA march (Coalisland to Dungannon) took place in August 1968. It was in response to a decision of Dungannon Council to give a council house in the village of Caledon to a nineteen-year-old Protestant woman. Although the police rerouted the demonstration, it passed off without incident.

House allocation was also the issue that led to NICRA's second march in Derry/Londonderry on 5 October 1968. Because of the threat of disorder, the Government banned the march, but it went ahead anyway and was met by violence from the police. Their heavy-handed tactics were captured on TV and beamed across the world.

Further NICRA marches made the situation even worse. Quite often, violence resulted. There were several reasons for this:

◆ NICRA going ahead with marches that had been banned by the Government.
◆ Marches were seen as provocative, especially when they went through Protestant areas.
◆ NICRA marches coming into contact with unionist counter-demonstrations.

Reforms

As a result of the unrest, O'Neill announced a five-point reform programme. It proposed:

◆ the allocation of council housing on a points system
◆ the replacement of Londonderry Corporation by a Development Commission
◆ the removal of parts of the Special Powers Act
◆ reforms within local government, including the ending of extra votes for business owners
◆ the appointment of an **ombudsman** to investigate complaints.

Despite the reforms, protests and counter-protests continued and so O'Neill appeared on television, appealing for calm. All further street protests were called off, but O'Neill still faced significant problems:

◆ The reforms had dismayed unionists who opposed concessions to the threat of violence and now felt that their position was under threat.
◆ O'Neill faced further opposition from within his own party, with Home Affairs Minister William Craig condemning O'Neill's television speech and arguing that the Prime Minister was acting under pressure from the British. Craig was sacked.

Tasks

1. Examine NICRA's early marches under the following headings:

	Coalisland-Dungannon	Derry/Londonderry
Date		
Reasons		
Outcome		

2. Create a spider diagram illustrating O'Neill's five-point reform programme.

3. Analyse O'Neill's television appearance and its aftermath under the following headings of (i) Reasons; (ii) Impact and (iii) Unionism Divided.

The People's Democracy March *WHAT YOU NEED TO KNOW*

There were a lot of reasons for O'Neill's resignation in 1969. You must be able to <u>identify</u> the different factors, <u>explain</u> them and <u>comment</u> on their impact.

People's Democracy

Although NICRA had called a halt to its campaign of marching, its decision was ignored by the recently formed People's Democracy. Made up mainly of university students, People's Democracy had developed demands similar to NICRA's:

◆ one man, one vote
◆ fair boundaries
◆ houses on need
◆ jobs on merit
◆ free speech
◆ repeal of the Special Powers Act.

Unhappy with the limited nature of O'Neill's five-point reform programme, People's Democracy announced that it was holding a march between Belfast and Derry/Londonderry in January 1969.

The marchers were attacked at Burntollet Bridge on the outskirts of Derry/Londonderry, an attack that the police seemed to do little to stop. Later on the same night, tensions were further raised in Derry/Londonderry when police rampaged through nationalist areas of the city.

The End of O'Neill

NICRA started to march again. The first march in Newry ended in violence. O'Neill responded by establishing the Cameron Commission to investigate the increasing violence.

This led to the resignation of two cabinet members, one of whom was Brian Faulkner. He argued that O'Neill was not strong enough to control the situation.

On 30 January 1969 twelve OUP MPs called on O'Neill to resign. Instead he called a general election – the 'crossroads election' – attempting to prove that public opinion was behind his efforts to modernise Northern Ireland.

The election took place on 24 February 1969. The result was not what O'Neill had wanted:

◆ there was a reduction in OUP support, and divisions of loyalty among the OUP MPs elected
◆ there was little or no support from Catholic voters
◆ O'Neill nearly lost his own seat to Ian Paisley.

O'Neill resigned on 28 April 1969. The final nail in his coffin was a series of bombings, which at the time appeared to be the work of the IRA, but which were actually carried out by loyalists in an attempt to force O'Neill to go.

O'Neill was succeeded by his cousin, Major James Chichester Clark, who had resigned from the Government less than a week earlier in protest at O'Neill's decision to introduce one man, one vote.

Tasks

1. Create a spider diagram indicating the aims of the People's Democracy.
2. Analyse the People's Democracy march using the following headings:

Reasons	Events	Results

3. Examine the 1969 general election using the following headings:

Why was it called?	
What were the results?	

4. Analyse O'Neill's resignation under the following headings:

Date	
Reasons	
Successor	

2005 Past Paper and Mark Scheme

(c) (i) Explain why the Civil Rights Movement emerged in Northern Ireland in the 1960s.

[6]

(ii) Explain why the civil rights protests led to growing violence in Northern Ireland in the 1960s.

[6]

(c) (i) Answers should refer to some of the following:
- Frustration at the failure of the Nationalist Party to address nationalist social and economic grievances.
- Formation of NICRA in January 1967 as a non-sectarian and non-political pressure group aimed at addressing political, economic and civil rights grievances.
- Key grievances were discrimination in employment; unfair electoral system in local government and lack of fairness in allocating houses.
- Emergence of educated Catholic middle class not prepared to accept this discrimination.
- Influence of USA Civil Rights Movement led by Martin Luther King. It used non-violent, **civil disobedience**, e.g. sit-ins, marches and rallies, and the media to successfully gain civil rights for blacks.

(ii) Answers should refer to some of the following:
- Ian Paisley organised counter-demonstrations to civil rights marches, e.g. Coalisland to Dungannon, August 1968. Unionists saw these marches as inconvenient and provocative.
- Government banned NICRA marches, e.g. 5 October 1968 in Derry/Londonderry. This led to clashes between the civil rights marchers and the RUC.
- Marches went through Protestant areas and were seen as provocative, e.g. the Burntollet Ambush in January 1969.
- People's Democracy, a more radical group, organised student sit-downs and the Belfast to Derry/Londonderry march broke the undertaking not to hold marches after O'Neill's Crossroads speech.

Section 2 Prelude to Direct Rule

The Summer of '69 *WHAT YOU NEED TO KNOW*

From mid 1969 onwards the political situation in Northern Ireland really began to deteriorate. One of the first political responses was the Downing Street Declaration and associated reforms. Make sure that you are aware of the key terms and reactions – specific contextual details are essential.

The change of leadership did not reduce tensions in Northern Ireland. Belfast witnessed an outbreak of house burning, mostly by loyalists. In Derry/Londonderry the annual **Apprentice Boys** parade on 12 August was followed by the 'Battle of the Bogside', which lasted for 50 hours. Finally, calm was restored by using troops to relieve the exhausted police; however, violence flared up elsewhere.

Government Reactions

On 19 August Chichester Clark met the British Prime Minister, Harold Wilson. The outcome was the Downing Street Declaration, which aimed to assure nationalists of equality of treatment, and unionists of the security of the union.

Further reforms followed:

◆ Electoral reforms, included 'one man, one vote' and an end to gerrymandering.
◆ A committee on policing was established under Lord Hunt.
◆ The Scarman **Tribunal** was set up to investigate recent disturbances.
◆ A single housing authority was established, taking over housing functions from local councils.
◆ Measures to prevent discrimination in public employment.
◆ A £2 million programme of work-creating schemes.
◆ Increases in investment grants.

Unionist Reactions

Many unionists were concerned at what they saw as continuing concessions to nationalists. The final straw came when the Hunt Report was published. It recommended:

◆ disarming the RUC.
◆ disbanding the B Specials and replacing them with the Ulster Defence Regiment, a part-time force under army control.

Angered at the proposals, extreme violence erupted on Belfast's Shankill Road.

Nationalist Response

Nationalists reacted positively to the reforms, believing that a positive future involving a reformed political system was now within their grasp.

Tasks

1. Analyse the violence of the Summer of 1969 using the following headings:

Location of violence		
Details		

2. Analyse the Downing Street Declaration using the headings of (i) Points to reassure unionists and (ii) Points to reassure nationalists.

3. Create a spider diagram identifying the various reforms that followed on from the Downing Street Declaration.

4. Complete the following table:

Unionist reactions to reforms	Nationalist reactions to reforms

Military and Paramilitaries *WHAT YOU NEED TO KNOW*

The split within the IRA, changing nationalist attitudes to the British army and the growth of Protestant paramilitary groups are all key developments in 1969–70. You need to be able to explain the details behind all of these changes and their political implications.

'I Ran Away' was the accusation most frequently levelled at the IRA because of its failure to defend Catholics during the violence of July and August 1969. Since the ending of its border campaign in 1962, the IRA seemed to have become more interested in **Marxism**. However, some of its members were unhappy with this situation and in the last days of 1969 the IRA split into two parts:

◆ The Official IRA (OIRA), which continued to focus on establishing a socialist Ireland. At the same time, it still used violence until a ceasefire was called in May 1972. In 1974, the movement split again with the emergence of the Irish Republican Socialist Party and the militant Irish Nationalist Liberation Army.
◆ The Provisional IRA (PIRA), which claimed for itself the traditional role of defender of the nationalist community. Its aims were:
  ◆ civil rights
  ◆ defence of the Catholic population
  ◆ the destruction of the Stormont Government
  ◆ the removal of 'British **imperialism**' from Ireland.

The IRA and the British Army

Initially, the British army was more acceptable to nationalists – as a source of protection – than it was to unionists. However, as the IRA's campaign began to take off, the army moved to protect itself. In July 1970, it imposed a 34-hour curfew on the Lower Falls area, while houses were searched for weapons. Although weapons were discovered, politically, the search was a disaster. It damaged the army's relationship with the nationalist community and helped increase IRA membership.

Protestant Paramilitaries

The Protestant paramilitaries sought a return to the old days of unionist domination. The UVF had grown and prospered against the background of NICRA's campaign and O'Neill's perceived **appeasement** of Catholics.

In September 1971, the UDA was set up. It viewed itself as a defensive grouping that would resist **republican** aggression. Within a year, it had over 30,000 members.

Faulkner

The levels of violence and destruction shot up during the remaining months of 1970 and on into 1971. There were attacks on the security forces and there was bombing of mainly unionist economic targets. In despair at London's inaction, Chichester Clark resigned as Prime Minister on 20 March and was replaced by Brian Faulkner.

Tasks

1. Explain the split in the IRA by writing a sentence beside each of the following:

IRA focus 1962–9	
1969 criticism of IRA	
Focus of OIRA	
OIRA use of violence	
Split in OIRA	
Role of PIRA	
Aims of PIRA	

2. Explain the change in nationalist attitudes to the British army by filling in the following:

Initial attitude	
Changed attitude	
Reasons for change	
Impact on IRA	

3. Analyse the change within unionist leadership in 1971 by completing the following:

Old Prime Minister	
New Prime Minister	
Reasons for the change	

New Parties WHAT YOU NEED TO KNOW

Questions on the emergence of new parties are common in the GCSE examination. Make sure you can explain <u>why</u> the changes took place, <u>who</u> was involved and <u>what</u> the new parties wanted to achieve.

Unionist Divisions

The depth of public dissatisfaction with the OUP became evident when Ian Paisley was elected as a Protestant Unionist to Stormont for the Bannside seat previously held by Terence O'Neill. Paisley followed up this success with his election to Westminster as MP for North Antrim in June 1970. In September 1971 his party was renamed the Democratic Unionist Party (DUP). Its aim was to defend the constitution of Northern Ireland while pursuing more progressive social policies.

April 1970 witnessed the launch of the Alliance Party, led by Oliver Napier. Although broadly unionist in its ideas, Alliance opened its doors to supporters from all denominations. It was hoping to achieve the parts of O'Neill's promises of reform not yet introduced.

Nationalist Divisions

Perhaps even more significant were the changes within nationalist politics. Eddie McAteer's old Nationalist Party had more or less faded away, and in August 1970 the Social Democratic and Labour Party was established. Led by West Belfast MP Gerry Fitt, the SDLP was moderately left wing on social and economic issues. At the same time, the party sought political reforms within Northern Ireland and the eventual re-unification of Ireland.

Task

1. Analyse the changes taking place within Northern Ireland politics at this time by completing the following table:

	DUP	Alliance	SDLP
Date of establishment			
Reasons for establishment			
Leader			
Policies			

Internment and Bloody Sunday *WHAT YOU NEED TO KNOW*

There are plenty of turning points within this course and internment is right up there in terms of importance. You need to be able to explain why it was introduced, why it backfired and how it then linked in with events that culminated in Bloody Sunday.

Internment

Brian Faulkner was unable to reduce the levels of violence and, facing strong unionist pressure for firm action to be taken, he re-introduced **internment** on 9 August 1971.

Internment failed spectacularly. The intelligence was entirely out of date; not one of the 452 men arrested was a leading member of the Provisional IRA. Moreover, despite the high levels of loyalist violence, all those targeted for internment were nationalists or civil rights supporters. The first loyalists were not interned until February 1973.

There were a number of responses to internment:

◆ Unionists were happy with the implementation of internment. They believed it had worked in the past and saw it as essential in ending IRA violence.
◆ Nationalists saw internment as one-sided in its application and open to substantial abuse.
◆ IRA membership increased.
◆ An orgy of violence and destruction followed the introduction of internment. Paramilitaries from both sides were involved.
◆ Along with other nationalist and republican Labour representatives, the SDLP called for people to withhold payment of rents and rates, and for a withdrawal from local government in protest at the policy.
◆ Civil rights marches were organised in protest at the introduction of internment, but the army's response seemed to be hardening. A protest held at Magilligan Internment Camp on 22 January was met with baton charges and CS gas from the army.

Bloody Sunday

In the aftermath of another anti-internment march in Derry/Londonderry on 30 January 1972, a riot developed. In response, troops from the Parachute Regiment shot 13 men dead; 13 more were injured, one of whom subsequently died of his wounds. An official inquiry headed by Lord Widgery failed to provide a satisfactory conclusion to the events of what became known as Bloody Sunday.

Apart from the immediate outpourings of grief and anger, Bloody Sunday had a number of results:

◆ continued support for the Government from the unionist community which, while regretting the deaths, saw the march as both illegal and provocative
◆ Catholic hostility to the state grew as symbolised by the burning down of the British Embassy in Dublin
◆ Britain faced international condemnation of the role that it was playing in Northern Ireland

◆ IRA membership increased

◆ the resulting increase in IRA violence and the Government's failure to end it led to the formation in February 1972 of the Ulster Vanguard. Headed by William Craig, the former Stormont minister, Vanguard was described as a co-ordinating body for traditional loyalist groups. One of its largest meetings, in Belfast's Ormeau Park, attracted 70,000 people.

Tasks

1. Examine internment under the following headings:

Reasons	Details	Reasons for failure

2. Create a spider diagram illustrating the various responses to internment.

3. Examine Bloody Sunday under the following headings:

Background	Details	Government response

4. Create a spider diagram illustrating the various responses to Bloody Sunday.

Section 3 Search for a Solution

Direct Rule *WHAT YOU NEED TO KNOW*

The reintroduction of Direct Rule was another key development. You will be expected to be able to identify the reasons <u>why</u> Westminster took this decision and explain <u>how</u> the different sides reacted to it.

Suspension

Faulkner demanded the power to rearm the RUC and re-establish the B Specials. Conservative Prime Minister Edward Heath responded by demanding control of law and order and justice; however, Faulkner refused. On 22 March 1972, Heath informed the Stormont Government that certain changes were being proposed, which included:

◆ the transfer of security control to Westminster
◆ the holding of a referendum on the future of the border
◆ the introduction of moves designed to allow the removal of internment
◆ the appointment of a Secretary of State for Northern Ireland
◆ the holding of talks with other parties in Northern Ireland in an attempt to establish a 'community government'.

Unable to accept the loss of control over the security policy, the entire government resigned. Heath responded by suspending Stormont and introducing **Direct Rule**. William Whitelaw was appointed as the North's first Secretary of State.

Reactions to the end of Stormont were predictable. Most unionists were horrified at the removal of Stormont. The last hours of the parliament were played out before a crowd of 100,000. This came in the midst of a series of massive protest strikes and shutdowns, organised by Vanguard.

The SDLP and the Dublin Government welcomed the chances for a new beginning. The IRA, although it had achieved one of its aims, stated its opposition to Direct Rule and announced its determination to continue its struggle to achieve a united Ireland.

1972: The Blackest Year

With 496 deaths, 1972 was the worst year of **the 'Troubles'**, even though there was a two-week IRA ceasefire. Some of the worst atrocities included:

◆ 21 July when the IRA detonated 20 bombs around Belfast in just over one hour. Nine civilians died on a day that became known as Bloody Friday
◆ 31 July when, without warning, an IRA bomb exploded in the village of Claudy. Nine civilians lost their lives.

The British Government responded with Operation Motorman, which reclaimed control of the paramilitary-controlled no-go areas established in Belfast, Derry/Londonderry and elsewhere in 1969.

Tasks

1. Examine the reasons for the introduction of Direct Rule using the following headings:

Faulkner's demands	
Heath's response	
Heath's demands	
Faulkner's response	
Changes Heath proposed	
Stormont Government response	

2. Create a spider diagram indicating the different responses to the suspension of Stormont and the introduction of Direct Rule.

3. Analyse Operation Motorman under the following headings:

Background	
Definition	

2004 Past Paper and Mark Scheme

(a) (i) Give **two** reasons for the suspension of Stormont and the introduction of Direct Rule in March 1972.

(ii) Give two reactions, one unionist and one nationalist, to the introduction of Direct Rule.
[4]

(a) (i) Any **two** of the following:
  - tension between Stormont and British Government over control of security policy and the army, especially after the events of Bloody Sunday;
  - the British Government was sensitive to international condemnation of its role in Northern Ireland especially after internment and Bloody Sunday;
  - breakdown of relations between Stormont Government and the nationalists. An opportunity for a new beginning to ease tensions.

(ii) Any **two** of the following:
Nationalists:
  - happy to see the end of Stormont and one-party rule. They welcomed the opportunity for a new system;
  - IRA opposed Direct Rule as an extension of British involvement and stated it would continue its fight.
Unionists:
  - anger and shock at the end of Stormont;
  - large demonstrations organised by Vanguard, up to 100,000 at Stormont. Strikes were called but had little effect.

Power-sharing *WHAT YOU NEED TO KNOW*

This can be a confusing period. You need to be able to explain <u>what</u> power-sharing was and <u>how</u> reactions to it undermined its chances of success. Equally important is your ability to explain <u>what</u> was agreed at Sunningdale and <u>why</u> the agreement was fatally flawed.

In March 1973, the British Government published its proposals for a new assembly (parliament). However, it was not to be given control over security or justice. There was also to be an executive (government). In addition, the British insisted that two other conditions would have to be fulfilled, for example:

◆ the sharing of power between Catholics and Protestants
◆ the formal recognition of an '**Irish Dimension**' – a role for the Republic of Ireland through the creation of a Council of Ireland.

Early Problems

Unionism was divided in its reaction to the plans. The extent of these splits became clear at the end of June when the results of the Assembly elections revealed that the number of **UUUC** (anti power-sharing) unionists elected was greater than the number of unionists elected who supported power-sharing.

The Executive

In November, Whitelaw announced that the power-sharing Executive would contain eleven ministries, all of which would go to supporters of power-sharing. Brian Faulkner would head the executive, while Gerry Fitt would be his deputy.

Sunningdale

The discussions about the Council of Ireland took place in December at Sunningdale in Berkshire. The meeting brought together the leading politicians from Britain, Ireland and Northern Ireland. However, there were no anti power-sharing politicians present: the Irish government and other local parties had argued that they would disrupt the negotiations.

After several days of negotiations, agreement between the parties was finally secured. The Sunningdale Agreement contained the following elements:

◆ London agreed not to oppose Irish unification if a majority of the Northern Ireland population desired it.
◆ Dublin accepted that Irish unity could only ever be achieved peacefully and with the consent of the majority of the people of the North.
◆ A Council of Ministers with fourteen members was to be established to help with the development of North–South co-operation.
◆ A 60-member Consultative Assembly would be elected by the Dáil and the Assembly at some future date.
◆ Also at some future date, control over internal security issues would be returned to the Assembly at Stormont.

Problems for the Future

On the surface, the Agreement looked promising; the problem was that the unionist and nationalist representatives believed that they had agreed to something entirely different:

◆ The SDLP saw the Agreement as paving the way towards the creation of closer ties between North and South.

◆ Faulkner saw it as a mere token, which he had agreed to as a means of getting Dublin to accept the position of Northern Ireland as part of the UK.

In addition, republicans were lukewarm in their support, seeing the new system as proposing substantially less than what they sought.

Tasks

1. Analyse the March 1973 British Government proposals for running Northern Ireland by writing a sentence about each of the following:

Key elements of the proposals	
Unionist response to the proposals	
Membership of the Executive	

2. Create a spider diagram showing the key points of the Sunningdale Agreement.

3. Analyse the key weakness of the Sunningdale Agreement using the headings of (i) Unionist understanding and (ii) Nationalist understanding.

The Executive in Operation WHAT YOU NEED TO KNOW

The chances of success for power-sharing – already slim – were further undermined by the 1974 Westminster General Election and by the UWC strike. Make sure that you can fully explain these important developments.

The Executive took up office on 1 January 1974. Almost immediately, its future was plunged into doubt:

◆ On 4 January, a meeting of the OUP's ruling body, the Ulster Unionist Council, voted to reject the Sunningdale Agreement. Faulkner resigned as party leader and was replaced by Harry West. As he retained the support of 19 of the 21 OUP Assembly members, Faulkner was able to remain as Chief Executive. However, it was clear that he had become isolated within unionism.

◆ On 28 February, a Westminster General Election took place. With 80 per cent of the unionist vote, eleven of the twelve Northern Ireland constituencies were won by the UUUC.

Strike

On 14 May 1974, a general strike began. It was organised by the Ulster Workers' Council (UWC), a group of Protestant trade unionists who had gained substantial amounts of political and paramilitary support. The aim was to show the levels of unionist opposition to the Sunningdale Agreement.

Initially, support for the strike was limited, but UDA intimidation and improved co-ordination by the UWC ensured that, by the end of the week, much of Northern Ireland had come to a standstill. Industries had closed down, there were regular electricity blackouts, fuel supplies were strictly controlled and there were hundreds of roadblocks.

The tension in the province was further heightened by the news on 17 May that car bombs, believed to have been planted by loyalists, in Dublin and Monaghan had claimed 27 lives (five more of the injured later died of their wounds).

Wilson's Fatal Intervention

Labour's Harold Wilson, the new British Prime Minister, was losing patience with the situation and appeared on television on 25 May to denounce the strike and call its organisers 'spongers'. This speech infuriated unionists and, more than anything else, ensured that the strike continued.

Although the British Government was not prepared to use the army to break the strike, it was prepared to use it to maintain fuel supplies. When the army was ordered in to take over fuel supplies, the UWC ordered a total shutdown. Seeing no obvious solution, and with the British and SDLP still refusing to negotiate with the UWC, Faulkner resigned as Chief Executive on 28 May. The other unionist members of the Executive resigned with him, thus ending power-sharing.

Having achieved its goal, the UWC ended the strike on 29 May. The Assembly was suspended on 30 May and Direct Rule was re-introduced.

Tasks

1. Analyse the initial problems facing the Executive by writing a brief summary under the following headings:

Faulkner's problems with the OUP	
Faulkner's position as Chief Executive	
February 1974 general election	

2. Analyse the UWC strike by writing a brief summary under the following headings:

Reasons for calling the strike	
Initial support	
How support increased	
Strike impact	
Bombs in the Republic	
Wilson's speech	
Army involvement	
Ministerial resignations	

2004 Past Paper and Mark Scheme

(c) (i) Why were many unionists opposed to the power-sharing executive of 1973–4?

[6]

(ii) Why and how did the UWC strike of 1974 lead to the collapse of the power-sharing executive?

[6]

(c) (i) Reference should be made to some of the following:
- Dislike of power-sharing with nationalists. Many saw Faulkner as betraying unionist principles.
- Sunningdale Agreement had set up a Council of Ireland. This increased Unionist fears about a United Ireland.
- Election February 1974, nearly 80 per cent of unionists voted for UUUC anti-power-sharing candidates.

(ii) Reference should be made to some of the following:
- Significant unionist support for the strike, though some evidence of intimidation by UDA.
- Effective role of UWC in co-ordinating strike, especially in controlling fuel and electricity supplies.
- Harold Wilson, British Prime Minister's 'spongers' speech hardened the resolve of the strikers.
- Failure of the British Government to order the army to intervene against the strike.
- Resignation of Faulkner on 28 May and downfall of the power-sharing executive.

Developments 1975–80 *WHAT YOU NEED TO KNOW*

While it is important to be able to explain the Constitutional Convention and the Peace People, the key development in this section is the removal of special category status and the IRA's reaction to it.

The Constitutional Convention

Britain's next attempt at a political solution was the 1975 Constitutional Convention. This aimed to allow local politicians to suggest their own solution. The Convention collapsed in November 1975 without agreement. The unionist parties proposed a return to majority rule with some minority rights. This was rejected by both the British Government and the SDLP.

New Security Policies

At the same time, the government pursued policies of Ulsterisation and criminalisation. The former involved reducing the strength of the army in Northern Ireland while increasing the size of the RUC and UDR. The latter saw the end of **special category status** for those convicted of terrorist offences.

Introduced in 1972, special category status had allowed those who claimed that they had broken the law for political reasons to live as prisoners of war. Its removal meant that those convicted after March 1976 would be treated in the same way as other criminals.

The Peace People

This period also witnessed the emergence of the Peace People. Led by Mairéad Corrigan and Betty Williams, the movement sought to use mass demonstrations to force an end to the Troubles. Although the efforts of the two leaders secured them the 1976 Nobel Peace Prize, they were unable to change the thinking of those involved in the violence and the movement eventually faded.

The 1980 Hunger Strike

IRA prisoners detested the policy of criminalisation. Their initial reaction to the removal of special category status was to refuse to wear prison clothes, instead covering themselves with blankets. This blanket protest was followed in 1978 by the dirty protest, when prisoners smeared their cell walls with excrement.

Public demonstrations in support of the protests met with little success. Even attacks on prison warders proved ineffective. Therefore, in late 1980, the IRA began a group hunger strike as a last method of achieving their demands. This was called off in December without anything having been achieved, although the prisoners believed that a deal had been made.

Tasks

1. Analyse the Constitutional Convention under the following headings:

Date	Purpose	Solution	Reaction

2. Analyse the Peace People under the following headings:

Leaders	Aims	Tactics	Outcomes

3. Analyse the IRA response to criminalisation by explaining the following terms:
- blanket protest
- dirty protest
- 1980 hunger strike.

The 1981 Hunger Strike WHAT YOU NEED TO KNOW

The 1981 hunger strike is yet another turning point. You must be able to explain <u>why</u> it took place, <u>what</u> happened and <u>how</u> it impacted on Northern Ireland politics.

Bobby Sands

On 1 March 1981 a second hunger strike began, led by Bobby Sands, the IRA inmates' Officer Commanding. This time, prisoners joined the protest at intervals so as to maximise its impact. However, although the hunger strike gained huge publicity it did not change government policy. Therefore, when the MP for Fermanagh-South Tyrone died, republicans put Sands up as a candidate. On the fortieth day of his strike, Sands, standing as an Anti-H Block candidate, was elected to Westminster.

Despite huge amounts of international pressure on both sides, neither side would compromise, and on 5 May Sands died. The strike continued until 3 October 1981, by which time nine other prisoners had died. In the same period, 61 people died as a result of violence in reaction to the deaths inside the prison.

Concessions Granted

No concessions were made during the hunger strike. However, within a week of the strike's end, James Prior, the new Secretary of State, announced that a number of the concessions that the prisoners had sought would be granted. These included:

- prisoners would be allowed to wear their own clothes
- the 50 per cent reduction in length of sentence lost by those involved in protests would be restored

◆ a greater number of prison visits would be permitted
◆ a greater degree of association among prisoners would be permitted.

These concessions resulted in the protests in favour of special category status all but ending by late October 1981.

Impact

The hunger strikes had a number of consequences such as:

◆ increased nationalist alienation from the state, resulting from what they saw as Prime Minister Margaret Thatcher's heavy-handed approach to the hunger strikers, whose demands they saw as reasonable
◆ the growth in support for the republican movement, which went hand in hand with increasing Catholic alienation from the state
◆ unionists – while glad that the Government had not given into the demands of the criminals on hunger strike – were increasingly voicing their anxieties at the seeming weaknesses of the province's security provisions
◆ the Irish Government was pushing for the introduction of a new political initiative to end the Troubles.

Tasks

1. Examine the 1981 hunger strike by completing the following mix and match exercise:

Leader of 1981 hunger strike	Fermanagh-South Tyrone
Constituency in which May 1981 by-election took place	10
Date hunger strike ended	October 1981
Number of prisoners who died	61
Number of people who died in related violence	None
Number of concessions made during hunger strike	Bobby Sands

2. Create a spider diagram indicating the concessions made after the hunger strike ended.

3. Create a spider diagram explaining the different reactions to the hunger strike.

The Rise of Sinn Féin *WHAT YOU NEED TO KNOW*

The growth in support for Sinn Féin, the concern that it caused and the Dublin Government's response are the important points for you to get to grips with here. However, don't forget to cast your eye over 'rolling devolution'!

Sands' victory in Fermanagh-South Tyrone showed the republican movement that there was much to gain from involvement in politics. That Sands' victory was not a fluke was proved when his election agent, Owen Carron, won the seat at the by-election following Sands' death.

The official endorsement of this policy came at the 1981 Sinn Féin ***Ard Fheis***. At this party conference, the delegates approved the movement's plan of contesting elections while also continuing to use extra-constitutional methods to achieve its aims. This became known as the 'Armalite and Ballot Box' strategy.

'Rolling Devolution'

The Government's next attempted solution was 'rolling **devolution**' – an assembly, which would be given decision-making powers only if there was cross-community support for power-sharing.

However, there was no real support for the initiative amongst the North's parties (with the exception of Alliance). Indeed, no nationalists ever sat in the assembly and it was finally dissolved in June 1986.

The results of the assembly elections clearly revealed the growth in support for Sinn Féin. Similarly, the party was winning seats in local council elections. Then, in the June 1983 Westminster General Election, the party's President, Gerry Adams, defeated Gerry Fitt for the West Belfast seat. The British Government was growing increasingly concerned that Sinn Féin might even replace the SDLP as the main nationalist party in the province, a prospect that also worried the SDLP. The party, led since 1979 by John Hume, was now looking more and more to Dublin for support.

The New Ireland Forum

That support was soon forthcoming. The New Ireland Forum was established by the Dublin Government in May 1983 to seek out possible solutions to the Northern Ireland problem. Attendance was limited to Ireland's constitutional nationalist parties. Sinn Féin was excluded, as *Taoiseach* Garret FitzGerald demanded that all participants reject the use of violence for political ends. Also, although they were invited, unionists refused to attend.

The Forum published its report in May 1984. It offered three possible solutions:

◆ A united Ireland achieved by agreement and consent.
◆ A **federal** arrangement, with parliament for the North within a united Ireland.
◆ Joint authority with London and Dublin having equal responsibility for running Northern Ireland.

Unionists rejected the Forum Report outright, while Margaret Thatcher's first public response came on 19 October, a week after an IRA attempt to kill her and senior ministers at the Conservative Party's annual conference in Brighton. The Prime Minister firmly rejected all of the Forum's proposed solutions and, for a time, Anglo-Irish relations deteriorated again.

Task

1. Analyse the New Ireland Forum by completing the following table:

Date	
Reasons for organising	
Who was there	
Who was not there (and why)	
Proposed solutions	
Unionist reaction	
British reaction	

The Anglo-Irish Agreement *WHAT YOU NEED TO KNOW*

There are three important areas for you to understand here: <u>why</u> the Agreement was signed, <u>what</u> it said and <u>how</u> different groups and individuals reacted to it.

The Anglo-Irish Agreement was signed on 15 November 1985. Historians have provided different reasons as to why it was signed:

◆ Constitutional nationalists in Ireland and the British Government feared Sinn Féin might become the principal nationalist party in the North. This would make the chances of agreement more difficult, could worsen the security situation and threaten the stability of Ireland.
◆ Thatcher realised that unless she dealt with nationalist alienation in Northern Ireland, she would not be able to improve the security situation.
◆ FitzGerald hoped that reduced nationalist alienation from the state and reform of the security forces in Northern Ireland would undermine the minority's toleration of the IRA and support for Sinn Féin.

The main terms of the Agreement were:

◆ Britain accepting that the Republic had a role to play in the government of the North
◆ the Republic accepting that a united Ireland was a long-term goal that would only happen with the agreement of a majority of the province's population.

The key structures set up by the Agreement were:

◆ an Intergovernmental Conference, headed by the Secretary of State and the Irish Foreign Minister. This would deal with issues such as security, legal matters, political questions and improving cross-border co-operation
◆ a permanent **secretariat**, based at Maryfield outside Belfast, made up of Northern and Southern civil servants to provide administrative support to the Conference.

Reactions

While the Agreement passed through both Westminster and the Dáil without any real problems, it met with a wide variety of reactions elsewhere:

Northern Ireland

Unionists   Unionists were appalled by the Agreement. They felt that they had been abandoned by their own government and believed that they were now in a process that would eventually result in a united Ireland. Only the Alliance Party did not condemn the Agreement outright.

Nationalists   The SDLP had been given more of a role in the creation of the Agreement than any other party in the North. It viewed the accord as an opportunity to create a better way of life for all those living in the province and welcomed the establishment of the Anglo-Irish Secretariat.

Republicans   Sinn Féin condemned the Agreement, arguing that rather than bringing a united Ireland closer, it actually 'copper-fastened' partition, since, in the Agreement, the Irish government was recognising the existence of Northern Ireland.

Republic of Ireland

The Fianna Fail opposition party led by Charles Haughey condemned the Agreement. Like Sinn Féin, Fianna Fail was dismayed at the recognition being given by Dublin to Britain's right to be in Northern Ireland. A prominent Irish Labour Party Senator, Mary Robinson, resigned from her party because the Agreement was unacceptable to the unionist community.

Britain

Ian Gow, a Treasury Minister, resigned from his position in the government. He argued that the Agreement was won by violence and would make the situation in the province worse rather than better.

Tasks

1. Analyse the Anglo-Irish Agreement using the headings of (i) Reasons why it was signed; (ii) Key terms and (iii) Structures established.
2. Analyse reactions to the Anglo-Irish Agreement by completing the following table:

Support		Opposition	
Who?	Why?	Who?	Why?

The Unionist Campaign of Opposition *WHAT YOU NEED TO KNOW*

Quite often examination questions will focus on <u>how</u> the unionist community attempted to destroy the Anglo-Irish Agreement. Make sure that you can identify <u>all</u> of the different method employed and can comment on <u>whether or not</u> they worked.

Unionist politicians decided that the best way of opposing the Anglo-Irish Agreement was by a campaign of non-co-operation with the British Government. However, they were also keen to demonstrate, by strength of number, the depth and breadth of unionist opposition to what they termed the 'Dublin **Diktat**'.

The campaign against the Agreement took a variety of forms:

◆ marches to the headquarters of the new Anglo-Irish Secretariat. On a number of occasions, the marches degenerated into violence
◆ a huge protest rally was held at Belfast's City Hall on 23 November 1985, attended by an estimated 100,000 people (some historians put the figure at as many as 250,000)
◆ all fifteen unionist MPs resigned their seats at Westminster, but then stood for them again in the resulting by-elections. The aim was to show the strength of unionist opposition through the total number of votes the candidates received. In the elections, unionists gained a total of over 420,000 votes but lost one of their seats to the SDLP. Significantly, Sinn Féin's share of the nationalist vote fell from nearly 42 per cent to just over 35 per cent. This suggested that one of the key aims of the architects of the Agreement – the destruction of Sinn Féin – might be achievable
◆ a unionist 'Day of Action' was arranged for 3 March 1986. Although much of the province was brought to a standstill using peaceful protest, in a number of places the protests resulted in violence
◆ the launching of a campaign of civil disobedience christened the 'Ulster says no' campaign. It included measures such as the shunning of British ministers; the refusal to set rates in unionist-controlled councils and a boycott of Westminster.

At the same time, a more sinister response was becoming evident. Loyalist paramilitaries engaged in a campaign of violence and intimidation against the RUC, who were seen as essential to the success of the Agreement. In addition, in November 1986, Ulster Resistance, a paramilitary organisation whose aim was the destruction of the Agreement, was formed.

Results of the Campaign

By and large, however, these tactics failed to have any impact on the British Government's determination to stick by the Agreement. The absence of fourteen MPs out of over 650 was not noticed at Westminster, and since local councils had little power as it was, the refusal to use this power made little or no difference. By September 1987, when the unionist leaders agreed to talk to British ministers again, it was clear that the campaign to destroy the Agreement had failed.

Tasks

1. Create a spider diagram illustrating the different ways in which the unionist community demonstrated its opposition to the Anglo-Irish Agreement.

2. Taking each method of opposition in turn, analyse why it was a success or a failure:

Method of opposition	Reasons why it was a success	Reasons why it was a failure

2005 Past Paper and Mark Scheme

(c) (i) Why did Britain and the Republic of Ireland sign the Anglo-Irish Agreement in 1985?

[6]

(ii) Explain the different reactions in Northern Ireland to the Anglo-Irish Agreement.

[6]

(c) (i) Answers should refer to some of the following:
- Dr Garret FitzGerald, *Taoiseach*, and the government in the Republic of Ireland supported John Hume and the SDLP. They had worked closely in the New Ireland Forum in 1983.
- The Irish Government wanted to improve relations with the British Government and undermine support for Sinn Féin among Northern Ireland nationalists.
- The 1984 Brighton Bombing and increased IRA violence in Britain convinced Mrs Thatcher that she must reduce support for Sinn Féin and the IRA among nationalists in Northern Ireland. Mrs Thatcher also hoped for better co-operation over security between Northern Ireland and the Republic of Ireland.
- Both Governments agreed to a role for the Republic of Ireland in the Government of Northern Ireland through a Secretariat of British and Irish civil servants. The Republic of Ireland agreed that unification could only happen with the consent of the majority of people in Northern Ireland.

(ii) Answers should refer to some of the following:
- All unionists were angry at the Anglo-Irish Agreement. They had not been consulted by the Conservative Government and felt betrayed.
- Unionist parties joined in organising a mass rally at City Hall in Belfast in November 1985. Up to a quarter of a million people attended. They launched a campaign of civil disobedience and an 'Ulster Says No' campaign. This campaign of opposition was a failure.
- The SDLP supported the agreement. It had been consulted by the Irish Government. It hoped to gain support at the expense of Sinn Féin. It welcomed the involvement of the Republic's Government in the Anglo-Irish Secretariat at Maryfield.
- Sinn Féin condemned the Anglo-Irish Agreement as 'copper fastening partition'. It resented the commitment of the Irish Government to give up its claim to Northern Ireland unless the majority consented.

KNOWLEDGE TESTS

Knowledge Test I (Pages 93–6)

1 Who did Terence O'Neill replace as Prime Minister of Northern Ireland?
2 How was O'Neill undermined by the method of his appointment as leader?
3 Name THREE policies introduced by O'Neill to improve the economy.
4 Name TWO economic successes.
5 Name TWO economic failures.
6 Name THREE measures introduced by O'Neill to improve relations within Northern Ireland and with the Republic of Ireland.
7 Who was the main unionist critic of O'Neill's political measures?
8 Give TWO reasons why there was unionist opposition to O'Neill's attempts to improve relations with the Republic of Ireland.
9 Name TWO cabinet ministers who opposed O'Neill's policies.
10 What evidence is there that some nationalists supported O'Neill's reforms?
11 Give TWO reasons why there was nationalist disappointment at O'Neill's reforms.

Knowledge Test II (Pages 97–101)

1 From where did NICRA take its inspiration?
2 Name THREE of NICRA's aims.
3 Name TWO groups that supported NICRA.
4 Give TWO reasons why some Protestants opposed NICRA.
5 Where was NICRA's first march from and to?
6 What happened during NICRA's second march?
7 Give ONE reason why NICRA marches often ended in violence.
8 Name TWO points from O'Neill's five-point reform programme.
9 Why did O'Neill appear on TV in late 1968?
10 Which group staged a march from Belfast to Derry/Londonderry in January 1969?
11 Where was this march attacked?
12 What was the Cameron Commission?
13 Which senior Cabinet Minister resigned in January 1969?
14 Give ONE reason why O'Neill was disappointed by the results of the 1969 general election?
15 Who replaced O'Neill as Prime Minister of Northern Ireland?

Knowledge Test III (Pages 103–8)

1. What was the 'Battle of the Bogside'?
2. What was the Downing Street Declaration?
3. Name FOUR reforms introduced in the aftermath of the Downing Street Declaration.
4. Why were unionists so annoyed by the Report of the Hunt Commission?
5. What names were given to the two parts into which the IRA split in late 1969?
6. Name TWO aims of the PIRA.
7. How did nationalists originally see the British army?
8. Give ONE reason why this initial attitude changed.
9. Which loyalist defensive organisation was set up in September 1971?
10. Who replaced Chichester Clark as Prime Minister of Northern Ireland in 1971?
11. Name TWO new parties set up in 1970–1.
12. What controversial policy did the Northern Ireland Government introduce in August 1971?
13. What happened at the anti-internment march held in Derry/Londonderry in January 1972?
14. Which British judge chaired an inquiry into the events of this day?
15. A meeting of which new loyalist group attracted a crowd of 70,000?

Knowledge Test IV (Pages 109–13)

1. How did the British Government react to the Stormont Government's refusal to hand over control of security to London?
2. Who became Northern Ireland's first Secretary of State?
3. Apart from Bloody Sunday, name TWO other atrocities that took place in 1972.
4. What was Operation Motorman?
5. What was the 'Irish Dimension'?
6. What was the UUUC?
7. How do we know that more unionists were opposed to power-sharing than were in favour of it?
8. Who were the top TWO Ministers in the power-sharing Executive?
9. Why did senior British and Irish politicians meet at Sunningdale?
10. What cross-border body was set up at Sunningdale?
11. On which date did the power-sharing Executive take up office?
12. How was Faulkner's position undermined in January 1974?
13. Why did the results of the 1974 Westminster general election undermine the power-sharing Executive?
14. What was the UWC?
15. Name the TWO locations in the Republic of Ireland that loyalist bombs exploded in May 1974.
16. What did the British Prime Minister call those people involved in the UWC strike?
17. What led to the UWC calling for a total shutdown in Northern Ireland?

Knowledge Test V (Pages 115–21)

1 What name was given to the 1975 attempt to provide a political solution to the Northern Ireland problem?

2 What was Ulsterisation?

3 What did the removal of special category status mean?

4 Name the TWO leaders of the Peace People.

5 Name the first TWO strategies employed by republican prisoners in an attempt to regain special category status.

6 Why was the first hunger strike called off?

7 For which Westminster constituency was Bobby Sands elected MP in May 1981?

8 What was the 'Armalite and Ballot Box' strategy?

9 What was 'rolling devolution'?

10 Who became MP for West Belfast in 1983?

11 Name TWO of the solutions put forward by the New Ireland Forum.

12 When was the Anglo-Irish Agreement signed?

13 Give ONE reason why the Republic of Ireland signed the Anglo-Irish Agreement.

14 List the TWO key terms of the Anglo-Irish Agreement.

15 Name TWO ways in which unionists opposed the Anglo-Irish Agreement.

Chapter 5 THE COLD WAR c1945–91

The Origins of the Cold War WHAT YOU NEED TO KNOW

Although most historians date the official start of the Cold War to 1945 there are many longer-term causes that you should be aware of.

The origins of the Cold War can be traced back to October 1917 when Lenin's **communists** seized power in Russia. This greatly worried western democracies as communism sought the destruction of the **capitalist** system that they operated.

Britain, France, Japan and the United States sent soldiers to help the communists' opponents in the **civil war** that followed the 1917 Revolution. The communists never forgot the fact that the capitalist nations had tried to destroy them.

This mutual suspicion continued and deepened throughout the 1920s and 1930s. It was made clear in a number of ways, for example:

◆ Russia was not invited to the 1919 **Paris Peace Settlement**
◆ Russia was not allowed to join the **League of Nations**
◆ it was not until 1924 that the British Government officially recognised the communist regime as Russia's Government (America followed suit in 1933)
◆ during the later 1930s, Britain and France refused to form an alliance with Russia against Nazi Germany.

Joseph Stalin succeeded Lenin as leader of Russia (now the USSR). When Britain and France failed to ally with Russia against Hitler, he signed a Non-Aggression Pact with the Nazis in August 1939.

Stalin and the Allies had to join together when Germany invaded Russia in June 1941. However, Stalin remained suspicious of the West, claiming that they delayed D Day until June 1944 to see if Germany and Russia would wear each other out.

Stalin was determined to ensure his country could never be invaded again. He therefore sought the creation of a buffer zone of communist countries between Western Europe and Russia as a way of protecting Russia from attack.

Tasks

1. Create a timeline illustrating the key developments in the Cold War before 1944.
2. Analyse the buffer zone using the headings of (i) Definition and (ii) Reasons.

Reshaping Europe *WHAT YOU NEED TO KNOW*

A big change in East–West relations took place between the Yalta and Potsdam Conferences. You must be able to explain <u>why</u> relations deteriorated so much. You should also be able to explain <u>what</u> was agreed (and not agreed) at these meetings.

In February 1945, Churchill, Roosevelt and Stalin (the Big Three) met at Yalta to discuss post-war Europe. It was agreed that:

◆ Germany and Berlin would be divided into four zones to be occupied by the Allies and France
◆ Germany would pay **reparations**;
◆ the United Nations (UN) would be established
◆ the USSR would declare war on Japan three months after Germany's surrender
◆ Poland would have new borders
◆ Eastern Europe would come under Soviet influence. However, it was also agreed that there would be democratic elections in these countries.

Potsdam

By the time the Big Three met again at Potsdam in July 1945, several changes had taken place:

◆ the war in Europe was over and Hitler was dead
◆ Soviet troops were spread throughout Eastern Europe
◆ plans were being made to return most US troops home
◆ Roosevelt had died and been replaced by Harry Truman, who was suspicious of Russia's aims
◆ Labour's Clement Attlee replaced Churchill as Britain's Prime Minister during the conference at Potsdam.

The meeting at Potsdam was much less friendly. Stalin's fear of the West increased when he was told that the USA had developed the atomic bomb, and that the Americans would not share the technology with the Russians.

At Potsdam, agreement was reached on:

◆ how Germany was to be divided and occupied
◆ how Austria was to be divided and occupied
◆ the reparations that each power could take from their own zone.

Tasks

1. Create a timeline illustrating the key developments in the Cold War in 1945.
2. Create a spider diagram illustrating the main decisions reached at Yalta.

3. Complete the following table, indicating the changes that took place between Yalta and Potsdam:

	Yalta	Potsdam
World War II		
US leader		
UK leader		
USSR leader		

4. Create a spider diagram illustrating the main decisions reached at Potsdam.

The Iron Curtain WHAT YOU NEED TO KNOW

The creation of the Iron Curtain, and the Western response to it, speedily resulted in the collapse of East–West relations. You will be expected to know which countries became communist and how they became communist.

Churchill clearly expressed the West's suspicion of Russia in a speech in Fulton, Missouri in March 1946. It was in this speech – in which Churchill condemned Stalin's attempts to control Eastern Europe – that the phrase **Iron Curtain** was first used. The speech helped to raise American awareness of the increasing tensions in Europe.

Stalin reacted angrily; he argued that having suffered 26 million deaths and severe economic and infrastructural damage, it was only natural that the USSR should want to protect itself from future invasion.

The Buffer Zone

Between 1945 and 1947 the following countries became communist:

◆ Albania
◆ Bulgaria
◆ Hungary
◆ Poland
◆ Romania.

In addition, communists held power in Yugoslavia, although its leader, Tito, a popular figure in his own right, was less inclined to do what Stalin told him.

Although the takeover of each country (apart from Yugoslavia) differed to some degree, certain trends were common to each, for example:

◆ pressure from Russia to secure key positions for communists in the temporary governments set up after the war. These positions were used to intimidate and imprison opponents
◆ suggesting radical changes to gain the communists popularity.
◆ controlling elections to ensure a communist victory.

Tasks

1. Create a spider diagram indicating which countries had become communist by 1948.
2. Complete the following table, illustrating the main steps that communists took to ensure control of Eastern European countries:

Step 1	
Step 2	
Step 3	

The Truman Doctrine and Marshall Aid *WHAT YOU NEED TO KNOW*

The ways in which the USA reacted to the spread of communism is crucial information. Make sure you are also clear about <u>what</u> Stalin's response was.

In March 1947 the British Government announced that it could no longer afford to continue funding the Greek Government in its fight against the communists. This worried Truman, who feared that if Greece became communist, so too would neighbouring countries and the fuel-rich Middle East.

Truman decided to ask **Congress** for help. He told Congress that it would be America's policy to use military or economic means to stop countries falling to communism either from external invasion or internal revolution. This policy became known as the Truman Doctrine. Congress released $400 million, which ended the communist threat in Greece.

Truman believed that communism spread more easily if countries were poor. He thought that if economic recovery took place in such countries:

1. Communism would fail to take control;
2. These countries would be able to trade with America, helping her economy.

US **Secretary of State** General George Marshall, agreed and proposed a massive investment of $13.3 billion into Europe over a four-year period (known as the European Recovery Programme, ERP). Initially, Congress was unconvinced; however, the communist takeover of Czechoslovakia in February 1948 changed its mind. Sixteen countries benefited from Marshall Aid, which was overseen by the Organisation for European Economic Co-operation (OEEC).

Stalin described the Plan as 'Dollar Diplomacy', arguing that America would use it to gain influence over countries by controlling their economies. He rejected the offer of finance and made sure that all the countries he controlled did the same by:

◆ establishing the Communist Information Bureau (Cominform) – this aimed to ensure communist nations worked together more closely and effectively
◆ setting up the Council for Mutual Economic Assistance (Comecon) – this was a Soviet version of the Marshall Plan, which encouraged economic co-operation among Iron Curtain states.

Tasks

1. Create a timeline illustrating the key developments in the Cold War, 1947–8.
2. Analyse the Truman Doctrine using the following headings:

Background	Definition	Congress's Response	Results

3. Analyse Marshall Aid using the following headings:

Aims	
Terms	
Congress's initial response	
How and why this response changed	
Impact of investment	
Stalin's response	

4. Analyse Cominform and Comecon as follows:

	Cominform	Comecon
Purpose		

The Berlin Blockade WHAT YOU NEED TO KNOW

The first potential flashpoint in the Cold War came with the Berlin Blockade. You need to know __why__ this happened, __what__ happened during it and __what__ impact it had on East–West relations.

Over two years after the end of the World War II, the former allies still had not reached agreement about the future of Germany.

◆ The Western powers wanted Germany to recover so it could be both a barrier against the further spread of communism and a cornerstone of European economic recovery.
◆ The USSR wanted Germany to remain weak since it had invaded Russia twice since 1914.

By 1948, the western zones of Germany were on the road to economic recovery, particularly assisted by Marshall Aid. However, Russia had removed a significant amount of resources from the eastern zone to compensate for war damage. As a result, living conditions there were much poorer.

By June 1948, the western zones had been merged, and the Allies decided to introduce a new currency – the *Deutschmark* – into the region. Stalin was concerned:

1. He saw this as the first stage in the reconstruction of a Germany, which would again threaten Russia.
2. This recovery would be obvious to the people of East Berlin, which could cause problems as discontent at lower living standards in the communist zone might develop.

Therefore, on 24 June 1948, and in violation of what had been agreed at Potsdam, Stalin ordered the closure of all road, rail and canal links with West Berlin. His hope was that the Allies would abandon the city and its two million citizens.

The USA was determined to hold on to West Berlin and decided that airlifting supplies to the city would be the best way of breaking the blockade. For almost a year, up to 13,000 tons of supplies were flown in daily, over two million tons in total. By mid 1949, Stalin was forced to admit defeat, and on 12 May the blockade was lifted.

The Berlin Blockade was a significant turning point in the Cold War:

◆ In April 1949, twelve western nations set up the North Atlantic Treaty Organisation (NATO). The reason was to ensure that the West could co-operate to prevent future Soviet aggression.
◆ The Warsaw Pact was established in May 1955 (after West Germany joined NATO). It was the communist version of NATO, with all countries in the Soviet sphere of influence agreeing to defend each other if one was attacked.
◆ In May 1949, the Federal Republic of Germany (known as West Germany) was established. In October, the USSR renamed its zone the German Democratic Republic (East Germany).

Tasks

1. Create a timeline illustrating the key developments in the Cold War, 1948–55.
2. Analyse the different attitudes to Germany's future, using the following headings:

Western attitude	Stalin's attitude

3. Analyse the Berlin Blockade by writing a sentence about each of the following headings:

New currency	
Living conditions	
Stalin's response	
US reaction	
Details of airlift	
Blockade end	

4. Analyse the results of the Berlin Blockade using the headings of (i) NATO, (ii) Warsaw Pact and (iii) Germany.

2003 Past Paper and Mark Scheme

SOURCE MATERIALS: THE BERLIN BLOCKADE AND AIRLIFT 1948–9

Source A: A view given in a British school text book

When the war ended in 1945 the USA played little part in Europe. Most American troops were sent back to the USA. In March 1947 President Truman announced a major change in American policy. The idea that the USA should help countries defeat communism became known as the Truman Doctrine. In effect the USA was taking on the role of the world's policeman in trying to stop communism spreading.

Source: J. F. Aylett: *The Cold War and After* (London 1996) p.8

Source B: A photograph taken in 1948 of West Berliners watching an Allied plane during the Berlin Airlift

Source: A. Todd: *The Modern World*, Oxford University Press, 2001

Source C: President Truman speaking in 1949

We refused to be forced out of the city of Berlin. We showed the people of Europe that we would act when their freedom was threatened. Our planes would fly in food and fuel as long as necessary. Politically it brought the people of Western Europe closer to us. The Berlin blockade was a move to test our ability and our will to resist communism.

Source: Adapted from B. Walsh: *GCSE Modern World History* (London 1996) p. 258

Source D: A Soviet view of the Berlin blockade

The crisis was planned in Washington, USA, behind a smokescreen of anti-Soviet propaganda. In 1948 the actions of the Western powers risked war. The self-blockade of the Western powers hit the people of West Berlin very hard. The people were freezing and starving. In the spring of 1949 the USA was forced to give in . . . their war plans had come to nothing, because of the actions of the Soviet Union.

Source: Quoted in P. Fisher: *The Great Power Conflict after 1945* (Cheltenham 1998) p.21

(a) **Study Source A.**
   What does Source A tell us about the changing attitude of the USA towards Europe between 1945 and 1947?

   [4]

(b) **Study Source B.**
   How does Source B support the statement by Truman in Source C about events in Berlin between 1948 and 1949?

   [6]

(c) **Study Source C.**
   How reliable and useful would Source C be to an historian investigating why the USA carried out the Berlin Airlift?

   [8]

(d) **Study Source D.**
   Source D says that the Berlin crisis was 'planned in Washington, USA'.

   Using Sources A, C and D **and your own knowledge,** explain whether or not you think this is a fair interpretation of the events in Berlin between 1948 and 1949.

   [12]

(a) Candidates may make the following points:
   • The USA played little part in European affairs when the war ended in 1945.
   • Most US troops were sent back to the USA.
   • In 1947 President Truman announced a change in US policy.
   • The USA would help countries to defeat communism.
   • the USA takes on role of world's policeman.

(b) Candidates may make the following points:
   • In Source C Truman claims that the USA would fly in food and fuel/act when freedom was threatened. Source B shows Allied planes in Berlin.
   • Truman claims they would not be forced out of Berlin; the photograph shows Allied planes in Berlin.
   • However, the photograph does not show what is in the plane.

- Brought people closer to us – people waving in support.
- Limitations of sources may be noted and can also be credited, e.g. only small number of people shown.

(c) **Level 1 ([0]–[2])**
A vague general account of the content of Source C with little attempt to address the question. Candidates at this level may discuss the content of the source but will not give any indication of the reliability and utility of Source C.

Level 2 ([3]–[5])
Answers at this level will discuss the reliability, utility and content of the source. Candidates may point out that it is primary evidence, i.e. dated 1949, clearly just after the crisis ended, and discuss the value of this. They may begin to make observations on its authorship and how this affects its reliability and utility.
- President of USA, USA perspective/view.
- Possibly one-sided US view only.
- Crisis a victory for West.
Limitations of source without discussion of reliability – Level 2 only

Level 3 ([6]–[8])
Answers at this level will discuss fully the reliability and utility of the source. Candidates should refer to the content and purpose of Source C and indicate how reliable it would be on its own as an analysis of US policy, i.e. one perspective only.

(d) **Level 1 ([0]–[4])**
Limited response, with a weak general answer which does not really address the question. Candidates at this level may accept Source D at face value and agree with its interpretation with little attempt to support this. May include some general points from own knowledge without reference to the source.

Level 2 ([5]–[8])
Answers at this level will indicate an awareness of the Soviet interpretation and contrast this with the American view in Source C. Candidates will make reference to the other sources to support their argument and may make use of their own knowledge. If more than one source is discussed and some reasonable points made, Level 2 mark should be awarded.

Level 3 ([9]–[12])
Candidates at this level will show a clear appreciation of the perspectives of each side as outlined in Sources C (USA) and D (USSR). Answers will be supported by the candidate's own knowledge and will include references to the other sources, e.g. Source A spells out the intention of US policy after 1947, which was regarded with hostility by the USSR. Candidates will set these interpretations in their historical context, i.e. the deteriorating relationship between the USA and USSR in these years.

China WHAT YOU NEED TO KNOW

The fall of China to communism was a massive development in the Cold War, turning it into a worldwide struggle. You need to understand in particular how the USSR and USA responded to the communist takeover.

Since the 1920s, Chinese communists, led by Mao Zedong, had been engaged in a civil war with Chiang Kai-shek's Nationalist Kuomintang (KMT). Despite significant American support for the KMT, the communists were eventually victorious. On 1 October 1949, Mao Zedong announced the establishment of the People's Republic of China. Chiang Kai-shek fled to the nearby island of Formosa (later called Taiwan).

The USSR was delighted that China was now communist. In 1950, a Treaty of Friendship was agreed between the two powers, which committed Russia to helping China's economic, technological and military development.

America was severely concerned by these developments, fearing that neighbouring countries would also become communist. This was called the **domino theory**. Americans also suspected that the fall of China was part of Stalin's scheme to spread communism across the world.

As it regarded Mao Zedong as little more than Stalin's puppet, the United States' Government:

1. Refused to recognise the new regime as China's legitimate government.
2. Tried its best to ignore communist China and continued to support Chiang Kai-shek's right to represent China in the UN.

Stalin's attempts to obtain the Chinese seat at the UN for the communists were rejected; in response, the Soviet delegation to the UN staged a walkout.

Tasks

1. Complete the following table about China before 1949:

Name of party/group		
Leader		
Position in 1949		

2. Analyse the response to the communist takeover of China by completing the following table:

	USSR	USA
Reaction		
Steps taken		

Korea (I): Before China *WHAT YOU NEED TO KNOW*

Korea is where the Cold War became hot for the first time. It is a complicated conflict and the progress of the war is hard to follow. Make sure that you can explain why it started and how it developed in its early stages.

Partition

In 1945, Korea was liberated from Japanese control by Russian soldiers who moved into the north of the country, and by American troops who landed in the south. The country was partitioned along the 38th parallel until elections could be held and the country reunited.

The elections were never held, and by the time the Russian and American forces had left Korea in 1949, two separate governments had been established to run the country:

◆ in North Korea, a communist regime was set up under Kim Il Sung.
◆ in South Korea, a capitalist dictatorship was established under Syngman Rhee.

Invasion

Both states sought the reunification of the country, and on 25 June 1950, North Korea invaded the south. Within days, the capital, Seoul, had been captured. The USA asked the UN to intervene to stop the attack. First it condemned the attack; then it began to put together a military force to stop the invasion.

Russia was unable to use its **veto** to object to the UN's actions as it was then **boycotting** the UN. This was in protest at America's refusal to allow communist China to sit on the UN Security Council.

The UN force – which was mainly American and led by an American general, Douglas MacArthur – landed at Inchon in September 1950. Before long, it had reached the 38th parallel.

Tasks

1. Create a timeline illustrating the background to and events of the Korean War, up to the UN's involvement.
2. Analyse the Korean War by explaining the following headings:

Korea 1939–45	
Korea 1945–9	
Invasion	
US reaction	
USSR reaction	
UN invasion	

Korea (II): China Involved *WHAT YOU NEED TO KNOW*

The war became much more dangerous once China became involved. Make sure you can explain why this happened, how the conflict then developed and what impact it had.

China

MacArthur did not stop at the 38th parallel. Crossing the 38th parallel meant that the UN force was now exceeding its UN orders. MacArthur's intention (with Truman's agreement) was to reunite Korea and 'roll back' communism. This worried North Korea's neighbour China, which feared that America would take the opportunity to invade China and restore Chiang Kai-shek.

MacArthur pushed on as far as the Yalu River, North Korea's border with China. Fearing the worst, over 250,000 Chinese troops invaded North Korea in November 1950 and pushed the UN forces back over the 38th parallel.

MacArthur now pleaded with Truman to allow a nuclear attack and an invasion that would lead to the destruction of communism in China. Truman however had decided on **containment** rather than confrontation, and refused to consent to an escalation of the conflict, fearing direct Russian intervention. In April 1951 MacArthur was sacked.

The war dragged on back and forth across the 38th parallel until the middle of 1951 when both sides dug in. The war then took to the skies, where US and USSR pilots fought for a further two years. The aerial battles were kept secret from the US population in case they demanded all-out war with Russia.

Peace talks started in June 1951, but were unable to find a solution acceptable to all sides. In 1953, Eisenhower succeeded Truman, and Stalin died, eventually leaving Nikita Khrushchev in control. The new leaders sought peace, and a ceasefire was agreed in July 1953. Although a peace treaty was never signed, the agreement saw the creation of a permanent border – slightly north of the 38th parallel – and a demilitarised zone (DMZ) between the two states.

Results of the Korean War

- ◆ Over two million died.
- ◆ Containment worked: communism did not spread into South Korea.
- ◆ The relationship between North and South Korea remained tense and bitter.
- ◆ US–Chinese relations deteriorated further.
- ◆ Realising the importance of preventing Japan falling to communism, America signed a peace treaty, ended military occupation and invested heavily in the Japanese economy.
- ◆ The USA signed agreements with the Philippines, Australia and New Zealand, which confirmed its position as the protector of the region.
- ◆ NATO was turned into a full-blown military alliance.

Tasks

1. Create a timeline illustrating the events of the Korean War after the UN force crossed the 38th parallel.

2. Analyse the Korean War by explaining the following headings:

UN campaign beyond 38th parallel	
China's reaction	
MacArthur	
Korea 1951–3	
Ceasefire	

3. Create a spider diagram indicating the main results of the Korean War.

Hungary WHAT YOU NEED TO KNOW

Events in Hungary were a test for the new leader of the USSR, Nikita Khrushchev. It is essential that you can explain <u>why</u> the rising took place, and <u>how</u> the East and West responded to it.

Khrushchev

Stalin's death in March 1953 was greeted by workers' riots in East Germany. By 1955, Nikita Khrushchev had emerged as the country's leader. Initially, a positive tone seemed to be set by some of the things that the new leader did, for example:

◆ in 1955 he visited Yugoslavia and apologised for the way in which Stalin had treated the country
◆ in 1955 he agreed to meet the leaders of the West in Geneva; the first such meeting for over a decade
◆ in February 1956 he delivered an historic speech (known as the Secret Speech) at the Communist Party's twentieth party congress, denouncing Stalin's policies and urging the development of 'peaceful co-existence' with non-communist nations
◆ he began a policy of ending Stalin's influence over the USSR (**destalinisation**).

Listening to Khrushchev, citizens of other Iron Curtain countries began to believe that a more relaxed system of government might emerge in their countries.

Unrest

Resentment of economic hardship emerged first in Poland in July 1956 when protests were held. Although Soviet tanks crushed the opposition, Khrushchev also agreed to the appointment of a moderate communist, Wladyslaw Gromulka, as leader, and to the introduction of a number of reforms. However, he insisted that Poland remain within the Warsaw Pact.

Unrest spread to Hungary, where years of bitterness at the hardships of repressive communist rule spilled over into a full-blown rebellion. The following events took place in late 1956.

23 October	Hungarian students took to the streets demanding reforms.
26 October	Imre Nagy, a moderate communist, was appointed as leader in place of the hard-line Matyas Rakosi.
1 November	Nagy announced that Hungary would hold free multi-party elections and would withdraw from the Warsaw Pact.
4 November and after	Over 6000 Russian tanks crossed the border to put down the revolt. Pleas for the West and UN to intervene were made. In the fierce fighting that followed the invasion, 30,000 died and a quarter of a million fled westward. Nagy fled to the Yugoslav Embassy but was later arrested and executed. He was replaced by Janos Kadar, and communist control was reasserted. At that stage, some reforms were introduced.

Russia's response indicated that she could not take the risk of a member of the Warsaw Pact leaving the organisation.

Throughout the crisis, the people of Hungary had hoped for assistance from the West; however nothing arrived except words of support. This was because:

◆ the Western powers were preoccupied and divided by the Suez Crisis
◆ the USA was in the middle of a presidential election campaign
◆ the West felt that it would be much more risky to confront Russia in Eastern Europe, which it now accepted as a Soviet sphere of influence, than it was to confront communism in Asia.

Tasks

1. Create a timeline indicating the main events leading up to the Hungarian Uprising of 1956.
2. Analyse the evidence of Khrushchev's moderation by filling in the following table:

Yugoslavia	
Geneva	
Twentieth party congress	
Destalinisation	

3. Analyse events in Poland in 1956 under the following headings:

Reasons	Events	Results

4. Analyse events in Hungary in 1956 under the following headings:

Reasons	Events	Results	Western reactions

The Berlin Wall *WHAT YOU NEED TO KNOW*

Berlin became a focus for the second time in the late 1950s. You will be expected to be able to explain <u>why</u> Khrushchev was concerned, <u>how</u> he responded and <u>how</u> the West reacted.

Although Berlin was a divided city, it was still possible for people to flee from the East to the West through West Berlin. It is estimated that by 1962 over two million people had done so. This worried the USSR as:

◆ it meant a significant loss of manpower
◆ it implied that people preferred capitalism to communism.

In addition, Khrushchev was concerned about West Berlin being used as a 'listening post', enabling the West to gain information about activities behind the Iron Curtain.

In 1958, Khrushchev attempted to force the West to withdraw by threatening to give East Germany control of access points to the city if the Western powers did not leave. His efforts failed. In 1960, he attended a **summit** meeting in Paris, again hoping to persuade the West to leave, but the meeting collapsed when Khrushchev revealed that Russia had shot down a U2 spy plane flying over its territory.

The events of 1960 increased tensions even further and a new wave of people fled through West Berlin, causing labour shortages in the east of the city. In August 1961 Khrushchev ordered the erection of a massive wall to divide the city. Armed guards patrolled the wall and those attempting to cross it without permission ran the risk of being shot. The river of defections dwindled to a trickle.

America protested and President Kennedy visited West Berlin to demonstrate his solidarity with its citizens. However, the USA did nothing more practical as it was unwilling to risk war.

Tasks

1. Complete the following table to explain Khrushchev's concern about Berlin:

Manpower	
Propaganda	
Security	

2. Using the following headings, explain the steps Khrushchev took to solve the problem of Berlin:

Step	Details	Result
Access points		
1960 summit		
1961 wall		

2005 Past Paper and Mark Scheme

2 This question is about Russian control over Eastern Europe between 1945 and 1961.

(a) Why did the USSR want to control Eastern Europe and how did it keep control between 1945 and 1961?

[18]

(b) How did the USA react to Russian attempts to keep control over Eastern Europe between 1945 and 1961?

[12]

2 (a) **Level 1 ([0]–[6])**
Simple descriptive answer which may be episodic and lack historical accuracy. To reach the top of Level 1, answers must attempt to provide some detail of some of the reasons why the USSR wanted to control Eastern Europe and of some of the methods used to do so between 1945 and 1961. Spells, punctuates and uses the rules of grammar with reasonable accuracy.

Level 2 ([7]–[12])
Developed but limited explanation which goes beyond Level 1 by providing a more accurate account of events and a more informed, if limited analysis. To reach the top of Level 2, answers must give specific details on the reasons why and methods by which the USSR kept its control over Eastern Europe. Spells, punctuates and uses the rules of grammar with adequate accuracy.

Level 3 ([13]–[18]
Well-informed, accurate account and a clear and coherent analysis of events. Answers must display sound understanding of the reasons why and methods by which the USSR kept its control over Eastern Europe. Answers may include some of the following:
- USSR need for security from Germany. 26 million Russians were killed in World War II, and its economy and infrastructure were badly damaged.
- In World War II USSR and the West were on the same side fighting a common enemy. USSR felt that USA and Britain delayed their offensive against Germany. Stalin was suspicious that the West had wanted USSR destroyed by Germany because of their dislike of communism.
- USSR wanted to create a buffer zone between Germany and USSR to protect it from future attack. USSR insisted that these countries were to be controlled by communist governments.
- The USSR army had 'liberated' the countries of Eastern Europe as it pushed the German army westward in 1944 and 1945. When Germany was defeated, the Russian army continued to occupy these countries and by 1947 it ensured that communist governments were imposed in Poland, Romania, Bulgaria, Albania, Hungary and the Russian zone of Germany. It used rigged elections, violence, imprisonment and deaths of opposition leaders, and promises of economic recovery. In 1948 there was a communist coup in Czechoslovakia. USSR control over Eastern Europe was complete.
- From June 1948 to May 1949 USSR imposed a blockade on all road, rail and canal links between the western zones of Germany and West Berlin. This broke the

Potsdam Agreement and showed Stalin's determination to remove the only Western influence behind the Iron Curtain.

- Strict political and economic control from Moscow was imposed on these countries through Cominform and Comecon. Contact with the West became more difficult as barbed wire fences, army patrols and lookout posts were built along the border with Western Europe. Churchill called this divide the 'Iron Curtain'.
- In 1955 USSR set up the Warsaw Pact, a military alliance controlled from Moscow to ensure that Eastern Europe remained under USSR control.
- In November 1956 in Hungary years of resentment at communist control led to the first serious challenge to USSR control of Eastern Europe. The unpopular pro-Russian leader, Rakosi, was overthrown. The new leader, Nagy, announced free elections and Hungary's intention to leave the Warsaw Pact. The new Russian leader, Khrushchev, reacted with force to crush this threat to Russian control over Eastern Europe. 6000 Russian tanks were sent to Budapest and the rebellion crushed. Thousands of Hungarians were killed and 250,000 fled to the West before Russian control was restored. Nagy was later hanged.
- During the 1950s, up to 2 million, mainly young skilled workers escaped from East Germany to the West through West Berlin. There was a labour shortage in the East and Khrushchev feared this would weaken Russian control. In August 1961 USSR erected a wall that sealed off East Berlin from the western sectors. The Berlin Wall did succeed in stopping the movement from east to west, but this concrete curtain became a potent symbol of the divisions in Europe and showed the lengths that USSR would go to keep its control over Eastern Europe.

(b) **Level 1 ([0]–[4])**
General narrative perhaps not addressing the question or offering little detail which may be accurate. Spells, punctuates and uses the rules of grammar with reasonable accuracy.

Level 2 ([5]–[8])
Answers at this level will address the question. Candidates will be aware of the ways in which USA reacted to Russian attempts to keep control over Eastern Europe between 1945 and 1961 but answers will lack sufficient depth and detail. Spells, punctuates and uses the rules of grammar with adequate accuracy.

Level 3 ([9]–[12])
Candidates will show a detailed knowledge of the ways in which the USA reacted to Russian attempts to keep control over Eastern Europe in the period indicated. Answers may include some of the following:

- From 1945 to 1947 USA withdrew its soldiers from Europe and took little active part in events in Europe. It only reacted when it realised that USSR had control over Eastern Europe.
- In 1947 USA began to take a more active role in the context of the Cold War. The Truman Doctrine was based on the belief that USSR was undertaking a worldwide communist revolution. This forced USA to take a more active role in containing communism.
- USA gave $400 million to prevent Greece and Turkey becoming communist. This

helped ensure the defeat of the communists in the civil war in Greece. In 1947 USA, through the Marshall Plan, gave $13 billion to help the economic recovery of Europe. USA believed that economic recovery and prosperity would make communism less attractive.

- USA undertook the Berlin Airlift to save West Berlin from USSR blockade from June 1948 to May 1949. Over 2 million tons of supplies were flown to West Berlin to provide food, fuel and supplies to the 2 million citizens of West Berlin. The Berlin Airlift was a test of USA's commitment to prevent the spread of communism as outlined in the Truman Doctrine.
- In 1949 USA set up NATO, a defence organisation of twelve Western countries to ensure co-operation against a surprise Russian attack. US nuclear missiles were installed in Western Europe. USSR viewed this as an aggressive action.
- In the 1950s, USA recognised the reality of the Iron Curtain and Eastern Europe as within USSR's sphere of influence. It did not risk confrontation with USSR. Thus in 1956, during the Hungarian Rebellion, USA did not send help to the rebels.
- In 1961 President Kennedy visited West Berlin to offer moral support but did nothing to prevent the building of the Berlin Wall.

The Cuban Missile Crisis (I): Origins *WHAT YOU NEED TO KNOW*

The Cuban Missile Crisis was perhaps as close to World War III as the Cold War came. Again, there is a lot going on, so try to identify the <u>reasons</u> for the fallout between the USA and Cuba, <u>how</u> the USSR got involved and <u>what</u> Kennedy's options were.

Castro

After Fidel Castro took over Cuba in 1959 he **nationalised** industries and banks, many of which were owned by Americans. As US hostility to Cuba grew and trade between the two countries declined, Castro turned to the USSR and, in 1960, they agreed to trade oil and sugar for machinery. In 1961, Castro announced that he had become a communist.

In January 1961, John F Kennedy became US President. Shortly after he took over, the **CIA** informed him that they were planning an invasion of Cuba. Kennedy approved the invasion, but it went totally wrong. The invaders had hugely overestimated the amount of support that they would receive from Cubans. The invasion – known as the Bay of Pigs disaster after the bay in Cuba on which the invaders landed – made Kennedy look inexperienced and turned Castro into a hero.

Crisis

Increasingly, Castro began to turn to Russia for assistance. This resulted, in August 1962, in the arrival of the equipment required to establish nuclear missile bases in Cuba. Missiles in Cuba would be able to reach most US cities and would provide a counterbalance to the US missiles that had been installed in countries such as Turkey (because of their proximity to the USSR).

US intelligence obtained proof of the missile bases by 14 October 1962. It also revealed that Russian ships were en route to Cuba with further supplies. Kennedy was determined that he would not be made to look foolish again.

Kennedy had a number of options:

1. Do nothing
2. Attack the bases by air
3. Invade Cuba
4. Blockade Cuba.

The President was helped to make his decision by a committee known as ExComm, a committee of the **National Security Council**. A key member was his brother Robert Kennedy.

Task

1. Analyse the background to and early days of the Cuban Missile Crisis by writing a sentence about each of the following:

Reasons for US hostility	
Cuba and USSR	
Castro and communism	
Bay of Pigs	
Missiles	
US options	

The Cuban Missile Crisis (II): Development and Resolution

WHAT YOU NEED TO KNOW

The Crisis becomes confusing as it unfolds. Make sure you can explain how it developed and how it ended. Finally you need to be able to assess which side won and explain the changes brought in after the crisis.

Standoff

On 22 October, Kennedy decided on a naval blockade of Cuba. On the same day, he revealed the unfolding crisis in a television broadcast. The remainder of the crisis played out as follows:

24 October	Beginning of the US naval blockade. US planes began to fly missions over Cuba. Upon reaching the naval blockade, the Russian ships were either stopped or turned away. Evidence from U2 spy planes suggested that the missile sites were nearing completion.
26 October	On the same day that tensions were increased with the shooting down of a U2 spy plane, Kennedy received a telegram from Khrushchev, which stated that Russia would remove the missiles if America agreed to end the blockade and undertook not to invade Cuba.
27 October	A second telegram arrived from Khrushchev. This stated that Russia would only remove its missiles from Cuba if America removed its missiles from Turkey. Against a background of advisers recommending an air strike, Kennedy decided to ignore Khrushchev's second letter and send a reply to the first one. In this, he agreed to remove the blockade and not invade the island in return for the removal of Russian missiles. He added that if he did not receive a reply by 29 October, an invasion of Cuba would begin.
28 October	Khrushchev agreed to Kennedy's offer and the removal of the missiles began.

Outcome

In public, it looked like a great victory for Kennedy; in reality, however, the result was not so clear-cut. Kennedy had secretly agreed to remove the missiles in Turkey. Shortly after the crisis ended, America began to dismantle some of its missiles from various bases in Europe including Turkey.

Several valuable lessons were learnt during the Cuban Missile Crisis. In particular, both sides realised how close war had been and agreed that such a confrontation should be avoided in the future. To assist with this, a telephone hotline between Washington and Moscow was set up. They also agreed to begin talks to reduce the number of nuclear weapons on each side. As a result, the Partial Test Ban Treaty was signed in 1963.

Tasks

1. Complete the following mix and match activity to explain the sequence of events during the crisis:

22 October
24 October
26 October
27 October
28 October

Blockade takes effect
Khrushchev telegram 1
Kennedy's offer accepted
Kennedy decides to blockade Cuba and announces crisis on TV
Khrushchev telegram 2
Kennedy responds to Khrushchev telegram 1

2. Explain the following:

Khrushchev telegram 1	Khrushchev telegram 2	Kennedy telegram

3. Who won the Cuban Missile Crisis? Complete the following table:

Reasons it was a US victory	
Reasons it was not a US victory	
Reasons it was a Soviet victory	
Reasons it was not a Soviet victory	
Reasons it was a Cuban victory	
Reasons it was not a Cuban victory	

The Vietnam War (I): Before Tonkin WHAT YOU NEED TO KNOW

In many ways, Vietnam is as complicated as Korea. Again, you need to be clear about the <u>background</u> to the conflict and the <u>reasons why</u> the USA got involved.

Vietminh

Since the 19th century, Vietnam had been part of the French Empire. During World War II, the Japanese replaced the French as occupiers. They found themselves under attack by the Vietminh, a nationalist army led by the communist Ho Chi Minh.

After the end of World War II, France tried to regain control of Vietnam, but the Vietminh resisted them. In 1950, the USA began to provide support for the French, seeing the conflict as yet another part of the ongoing struggle against communism.

In 1954 the French were defeated at Dien Bien Phu. This was followed by an armistice in which Vietnam was temporarily divided along the 17th parallel. The northern part would be under Vietminh control while the anti-communist Ngo Dinh Diem would control the south. It was agreed that, after elections were held, the country would be reunited.

US Involvement

The elections never took place, as the South Vietnamese government – supported by the US – were afraid that the communists would win. Washington also feared that neighbouring countries would become communist, creating a new communist power bloc based around China.

President Eisenhower provided financial and military support for the South Vietnamese government. His successor, John F Kennedy, increased the levels of aid. All this came at a time of increasing *guerrilla* attacks against the South's army by the National Liberation Front (NLF) or Vietcong. This group had been set up in 1960 to reunite the country under communist control. It was supported by Ho Chi Minh.

Ngo Dinh Diem was an unpopular leader. His regime was brutal and corrupt, and the government was made up of mostly Catholic landowners and was out of touch with its people, the majority of whom were Buddhist peasants. In November 1963, Diem was overthrown and assassinated by the Vietcong. By then, there were 16,000 US military advisers in Vietnam.

Tasks

1. Create a timeline illustrating the background to and early stages of the Vietnam War.
2. Analyse the background to and early stages of the Vietnam War by explaining the following headings:

Vietnam before 1939	
Vietnam 1939–45	
Vietnam 1945–54	
Armistice	
No election?	
NLF and US involvement	
Ngo Dinh Diem	

The Vietnam War (II): Escalation and Retreat *WHAT YOU NEED TO KNOW*

Why and *how* the USA increased its involvement, the *impact of* the war in Vietnam and in the USA, *how* it ended and *what* its results were are the key issues for you to gain an understanding of here.

Tonkin

In August 1964 the North Vietnamese attacked a US destroyer in the Gulf of Tonkin. Kennedy's successor, Lyndon B Johnson, believed that this provided the excuse for massive American involvement in Vietnam. The US Congress agreed, and passed the Tonkin Resolution, allowing Johnson to fight a war as he saw fit.

Over the next three years, massive numbers of troops were deployed while the US Air Force launched repeated bombing raids (Operation Rolling Thunder) against the Vietcong. In particular, the USA used chemicals such as Napalm and Agent Orange in their bombing raids. The former burned civilians indiscriminately; the latter cleared the forests of foliage. This enabled the Americans to see their enemy from the air; however, it also destroyed the land and wounded countless civilians.

With over 500,000 troops in Vietnam by 1968, the USA should have had no difficulty in defeating its enemy. However, the expected victory did not happen.

◆ The Vietnamese had already seen off two foreign armies.
◆ The US army was made up of many inexperienced soldiers (**conscripts**) and was fighting an enemy that used guerrilla tactics, dressed in the same way as the Vietnamese peasantry and knew the country well.
◆ The Vietcong developed a vast network of underground tunnels to support their guerrilla campaign.
◆ The Vietnamese people had no reason to support the US forces. US tactics, such as gathering peasants into large villages (Strategic Hamlets), annoyed many, while the army seemed prepared to harass and kill civilians in their efforts to root out the Vietcong. The most notorious example of this was the My Lai massacre of March 1968 when a large number of Vietnamese villagers were massacred by US troops.

In January 1968 the Vietcong launched a massive counteroffensive, getting as far as the South's capital, Saigon, before they were driven back. Although, ultimately, a failure militarily, the Tet Offensive began to make the Americans feel that they could not win this war.

Exit Strategy

The same feelings were beginning to emerge back in the United States where television pictures showed Americans much of what was going on. More and more young Americans were being drafted (conscripted), and more and more US troops were being brought home in body bags. Complaints were heard about the cost of the war. Students protested against the US Government's policies. Johnson himself became so unpopular that he decided not to run for re-election in 1968. The protests continued after Richard M Nixon became President. Four demonstrators were shot by the military at Kent State University. Even serving soldiers began to protest.

Nixon was determined to remove the US from the Vietnam War without it looking as if it had lost. To this end, he:

◆ increased the levels of bombing against North Vietnam
◆ ordered secret bombing raids against the neighbouring countries of Cambodia and Laos in 1970. This was because they were being used as supply routes by the Vietcong (the so-called Ho Chi Minh Trail)
◆ introduced the policy of **Vietnamisation**. By this, US troops would be withdrawn and South Vietnamese forces would do the fighting.

In 1973 a peace treaty was signed. Its terms allowed for the withdrawal of the US forces and the return of US POWs. It also allowed the Vietcong to remain in the South and put off a decision on the country's political future until a later date. Nixon felt able to argue that he had achieved 'peace with honour' but, by 1975, all of Vietnam was in the hands of the communists.

Results
◆ There were huge military and civilian losses.
◆ Many of the US veterans suffered severe mental damage.
◆ Vietnam was devastated by the war.
◆ Cambodia and Laos also became communist, although no other neighbouring country did.
◆ The USA spent at least $120 billion on the war.
◆ The war proved that an enemy that used suitable tactics could humble the USA.
◆ The policy of containment seemed to have failed.

Tasks
1. Create a timeline illustrating the events of the Vietnam War after the Tonkin Resolution.
2. Analyse the Vietnam War by explaining the following headings:

Tonkin Resolution	
US tactics	
Problems defeating Vietcong	
Tet Offensive and impact of war in USA	
Nixon's tactics	
Peace with Honour?	

3. Create a spider diagram illustrating the results of the Vietnam War.

The Czech Rising *WHAT YOU NEED TO KNOW*

There are some similarities between events in Hungary in 1956 and in Czechoslovakia in 1968. Make sure that you are able to explain <u>why</u> the reforms were introduced, <u>why</u> the Warsaw Pact was so concerned, <u>how</u> they acted, <u>how</u> their actions were justified and <u>how</u> the West responded.

Dubček

In January 1968 Czechoslovakia's hard-line leader Antonin Novotny was replaced by the more moderate Alexander Dubček. The reason for this was a series of demonstrations at the lack of civil rights and the appalling standard of living in the country, which had resulted from two decades of communist rule.

Dubček wanted Czechoslovakia to remain communist but he also knew that if that was to happen, reforms were needed. To achieve 'socialism with a human face' he introduced the following:

◆ freedom of speech and of the press
◆ less centralised economic control
◆ development of foreign trade
◆ removal of restrictions on travel abroad
◆ reduction in the powers of the secret police.

These reforms were greeted with widespread public approval. The new atmosphere produced by the reforms was christened the 'Prague spring'.

Invasion

Dubček's reforms were less enthusiastically greeted in Moscow. Leonid Brezhnev, the USSR's new leader, and the leaders of other Iron Curtain countries feared that the reforms would ultimately result in the destruction of the Iron Curtain. Dubček assured them of his commitment to socialism, and guaranteed that Czechoslovakia would remain in the Warsaw Pact.

On 20 August 1968, Brezhnev ordered 400,000 troops into the country, claiming that senior Czech communists had invited them in. Realising that opposition would be pointless, Dubček urged people to show their opposition through **passive resistance**.

Dubček was summoned to Moscow; on his return to Prague he announced that the 'Prague spring' had ended. He resigned a few months later and was replaced by the much more hard-line Gustav Husak.

Brezhnev Doctrine

Brezhnev justified his actions by arguing that it was the duty of communist countries to act together to prevent another communist state from turning to capitalism. This became known as the Brezhnev Doctrine.

The West responded with little more than words of sympathy. America, in particular, was too caught up with its own problems in Vietnam and accepted that there was no point in trying to intervene in events behind the Iron Curtain. It was also keen not to damage the recent improvement in relations between East and West that became known as *détente*.

Tasks

1. Analyse the background to the Czech Rising by writing about the following:

Date of Dubček's appointment	
Reasons for Dubček's appointment	
Dubček's aims	
Dubček's policies	
Public reaction	

2. Analyse the Warsaw Pact reaction to Dubček's policies under the headings of (i) Fear and (ii) Reaction.

3. Examine events following the Warsaw Pact invasion by commenting on the following headings:

Czech reaction to invasion	Dubček's fate	Brezhnev Doctrine	Response of the West

Détente WHAT YOU NEED TO KNOW

There was a thaw in the Cold War in the 1970s during the period of détente. The reasons for détente are tied up in the complicated relationships between the USA, USSR and China. Make sure that you understand <u>why</u> each country followed the policy, <u>what forms</u> it took and <u>why</u> it finally ended.

Origins

For part of the 1960s and most of the 1970s there was an improvement in relations between East and West. This improvement became known as *détente*. *Détente* emerged for a number of reasons, including the strained relations that existed between Russia and China by the late 1960s. Part of the US reasoning behind *détente* was her desire to take advantage of these tensions. America believed that if she could create better relations with China, this would put significant pressure on the USSR. She also believed that both countries might help her end the Vietnam War by putting pressure on North Vietnam to negotiate a settlement.

Sino-Soviet relations had deteriorated for a number of reasons:

◆ Differences over methods of agricultural development.
◆ China believed Russia wanted to dominate her.
◆ Russia refused to share nuclear technology.
◆ China was against Khrushchev's public criticism of Stalin.
◆ China believed peaceful co-existence was a betrayal of the ideas of Marx and Lenin. It thought Khrushchev was being too soft with the West.
◆ China condemned the Soviet climbdown over Cuba.
◆ In 1969 a border dispute between the two powers resulted in the deaths of a number of military personnel.

By the late 1960s, relations between the two states were at an all-time low. At the same time, China and the USA began to realise that there could be benefits from an improved relationship. In particular:

◆ economic advantages such as the opening of new markets to both countries and, in China's case, the possibility of the investment of capital and technological knowledge
◆ military benefits, in that the USA wanted China to put pressure on North Vietnam to negotiate an end to the Vietnam War
◆ diplomatic benefits that meant each country could use the other in their ongoing power struggles with the USSR.

Improved Relations

There were a number of stages in the improvement of relations:

1971	The US table tennis team was invited to visit China.
1971	China joined the UN.
1972	Nixon visited China.
1972	US–China Friendship Treaty.
1978	The USA granted China full diplomatic recognition.

Russia was concerned about the improvement in US–Chinese relations. Russia's desire to keep China isolated was one of its main reasons for wanting to improve relations with the USA, but there were other issues for both sides, including:

◆ the realisation that they had come too close to nuclear war in the 1960s and that new understandings needed to be reached
◆ the need to cut back on military spending due to the fact that both were facing severe economic problems
◆ America needed new export markets and Russia needed foreign supplies of grain.

A series of summit meetings were held between Russia and America at which the following key agreements were made:

Date	Name of agreement	Key details	Results
1972	Strategic Arms Limitation Talks (SALT I)	Limited the number of certain types of weapons.	Only certain types of weaponry were included; many more powerful missiles were left out.
1975	Helsinki Agreement	Acceptance of existing borders in Europe by USA. Agreement to improve human rights by USSR.	Human rights did not really improve behind the Iron Curtain.
1979	SALT II	Further limitations on weaponry.	Never approved by the US Congress because of Russia's invasion of Afghanistan in December 1979.

Tasks

1. Create a timeline to illustrate the history of *détente*.
2. Create a spider diagram to explain the reasons for the deterioration in Sino-Soviet relations.
3. Complete the following table to explain the benefits China and the USA saw in improving relations:

Economic	
Military	
Diplomatic	

4. Complete the following table to explain the reasons why Russia and the USA wanted to improve relations with each other:

China	
War	
Spending	
Exports	

5. Analyse the strengths and weaknesses of the various détente agreements signed:

	SALT I	Helsinki Agreement	SALT II
Strengths			
Weaknesses			

Afghanistan *WHAT YOU NEED TO KNOW*

The USSR had its own version of Vietnam with Afghanistan. You will be expected to know <u>why</u> the invasion happened, <u>how</u> the USA in particular reacted to it and <u>why</u> and <u>how</u> the conflict came to an end.

Invasion

On Christmas Day 1979 Soviet troops invaded Afghanistan. Brezhnev had decided to get involved more directly for two reasons:

◆ Moscow wanted to restore a government friendly to the USSR. The current government, while previously pro-Soviet, had developed links with the USA.
◆ More importantly, the Russians feared that if the Muslim rebels in Afghanistan – the **Mujaheddin** – succeeded in seizing control it might encourage **Muslims** living in the Asian areas of the USSR to try to gain freedom from Soviet control.

Before long, there were over 100,000 Russian troops in the country.

Reactions

Russia claimed that it had been invited into Afghanistan to help restore order, but few believed this. US President Carter was outraged by the invasion, coming as it did during the period of *détente*. His immediate response was to impose **sanctions,** by stopping US grain exports to Russia. The US Congress also took action and refused to approve the SALT II Agreement. In addition, Carter authorised an increase in arms spending. The USA also organised a **boycott** of the 1980 Moscow Olympic Games. Athletes from over 60 nations stayed away.

Despite their superiority, the Russian forces were unable to defeat the rebels who were using guerrilla tactics. This failure was particularly obvious to Mikhail Gorbachev who became leader of the Soviet Union in 1985. He realised how unpopular the war had become at home and how damaging it was to Russia's economy. He was therefore determined to end it. By February 1989, all Soviet troops had been withdrawn.

Results

◆ Afghan cities were left ruined and the countryside was made impassable due to landmines.
◆ Out of a population of 15 million, the conflict left 5 million homeless.
◆ The war cost 20,000 Soviet lives.
◆ Well over 1 million Afghanis died.
◆ The war drained huge amounts of money out of the Soviet economy.

Tasks

1. Analyse the Soviet–Afghan War by filling in the following table:

Dates of war	
Soviet excuse for invasion	
Real reasons for Soviet invasion	
US reaction	
Problems defeating rebels	
Reasons USSR withdrew	

2. Create a spider diagram illustrating the results of the Soviet–Afghan War.

America and Russia *WHAT YOU NEED TO KNOW*

During the 1980s, Cold War tensions worsened severely and then began to ease to the extent that the conflict was over by the end of the decade. Examiners will expect you to be able to explain <u>why</u> the relationships deteriorated so badly and then <u>how</u> they improved so much within such a short period of time.

Reagan

In November 1980 Ronald Reagan was elected US President. In 1983 Reagan christened the USSR the 'evil empire' and stated his determination to ensure that America would never be destroyed by communism. To this end, he began to spend huge amounts of money on new defence systems. A range of up-to-date missiles was introduced, many of which were based in Europe.

In 1983 Reagan announced the development of the Strategic Defence Initiative (SDI). Nicknamed 'Star Wars', it was a laser defence system that would effectively create a shield around the USA, which could not be penetrated by Russian missiles.

'Star Wars' cost billions of dollars and, before long, the US economy was in difficulty. However, the situation was even worse in Russia; as Moscow tried to keep up with USA, the already crumbling Russian economy came close to total collapse. Both countries needed to reduce costs as a matter of urgency.

Gorbachev's Foreign Policy

The state of the Russian economy particularly concerned Mikhail Gorbachev, who became Soviet leader in 1985. He knew that Russia could not afford to spend money in a vain attempt to keep up with US defence spending:

◆ Living standards were appallingly low.
◆ There were significant levels of corruption within the Communist Party.

◆ Millions were on the verge of starvation because of the poor performance of the agricultural sector.
◆ Much of Russia's industry was in dire need of modernisation.
◆ Technologically, Russia was decades behind the West.
◆ The war in Afghanistan was draining billions from the economy.

Gorbachev knew that economic reform in Russia would have to be preceded by huge cuts in defence spending. That would require a better relationship with the West. In 1986 he signalled a major change in Soviet foreign policy when he indicated Russia's desire to get rid of all nuclear weapons. He also indicated his willingness to abandon previous policies, such as the Brezhnev Doctrine, in favour of ensuring the security of the USSR. This meant that the buffer zone was no longer necessary.

In an attempt to reach agreement, Reagan and Gorbachev held a series of summit meetings. After intensive negotiations, both sides agreed to a reduction in weaponry. Their agreement was contained in the 1987 INF (Intermediate Nuclear Forces) Treaty. A year later, Gorbachev announced the withdrawal of Soviet forces from Afghanistan and a huge reduction in the size of the Soviet armed forces. Troops were also withdrawn from other Iron Curtain countries.

Under Reagan's successor, George H Bush (elected 1988), the changes continued. Bush was particularly impressed by the political changes that Gorbachev was introducing behind the Iron Curtain. He met Gorbachev in Malta in 1989, and both leaders declared that the Cold War was over. In July 1991 the Warsaw Pact was dissolved.

Tasks

1. Create a timeline illustrating the main developments in US–USSR relations, 1980–91.
2. Analyse the US approach to the Cold War in the early 1980s by writing a sentence about each of the following:

Reagan and the USSR	
New missiles	
'Star Wars'	

3. Create a spider diagram illustrating the problems facing the Soviet economy at this time.

4. Analyse Gorbachev's foreign policy under the following headings:

Reason for changing foreign policy	Changes introduced	Results

Glasnost and Perestroika WHAT YOU NEED TO KNOW

The different phases of the collapse of the Iron Curtain can be complicated. You need to understand <u>what</u> reforms Gorbachev brought in, <u>why</u> he did so and <u>what</u> their impact was in the different countries across the region. Be aware also of <u>what</u> was going on in China and <u>how</u> communism finally came to an end in the USSR.

Reform

Gorbachev began to encourage Russians to offer constructive criticism of the communist system as a way of helping it to modernise and improve. He stated that his reforms would revolve around the ideas of *perestroika* and *glasnost*:

◆ **Perestroika** restructuring of the Russian economy through the introduction of more western-style policies.
◆ **Glasnost** openness; in other words, there would be freedom to debate, freedom for the media, freedom from government control.

The people of the other Iron Curtain countries watched the changes in Russia with great interest. Gorbachev's decision to loosen the bonds that tied them to Russia and his refusal to force countries to remain communist meant that similar freedoms were now within their own grasp. Nationalist movements emerged as people sought their freedom. In each country, the search for freedom took a slightly different path.

Country	Key dates	Events
East Germany	1989	October: Gorbachev visited East Berlin and encouraged people to push for democracy. October: East Germany's leader, Erich Honecker, resigned. November: Berlin Wall opened, allowing freedom of movement between East and West Berlin.
	1990	October: Germany was reunified.
Bulgaria	1989	February: Free trade union established. November: Communist leadership resigned.
Romania	1989	December: After authorising the killings of large numbers of people protesting for food, dictator Nicolae Ceausescu fled. Later he was executed by the army.
Poland	1980	Solidarity set up as the first free trade union within the Iron Curtain. It emerged as a result of opposition to Poland's economic and political decline. Solidarity soon had 9 million members. Government recognised Solidarity.
	1981	Under pressure from Moscow, Poland's leader, General Jaruzelski, declared martial law. Solidarity was declared illegal but continued to exist underground, supported particularly by the Catholic Church and its Polish leader, Pope John Paul II.

	1989	April: Solidarity legalised again after a wave of strikes. Workers granted the right to strike. June: Solidarity won Poland's elections. August: A non-communist government installed. December: Lech Walesa elected President – the first non-communist leader in Eastern Europe for four decades.
Czechoslovakia	1989	May: Huge protest rallies demanded change. November: After some initial resistance, the communist regime was overthrown with almost no loss of life. This became known as the 'Velvet Revolution'. December: The Chairman of the newly elected federal parliament was Alexander Dubček. Playwright Vaclav Havel became President.
	1993	Czechoslovakia split into Czech Republic and Slovakia.
Hungary	1988	Hard-line leader Janos Kadar sacked. Imre Nagy given a state funeral.
	1989	January: Opposition parties allowed. March: Demonstrations held against Soviet troops. May: Fences cutting off the border with Austria removed. As a result, many East Germans went through Hungary and Austria into West Germany. October: A non-communist government set up.
Baltic States	1990	Initially, even Gorbachev resisted the demands of Latvia and Lithuania for freedom, as he feared that it would lead all the other republics that made up the USSR to seek the same: something he was anxious to prevent.
	1991	Estonia, Latvia and Lithuania declared their independence.
Yugoslavia	1980	Death of Tito.
	1990	Emergence of four different regimes within Yugoslavia.
	1991–5	A series of wars fought among the various ethnic groups in the region.

However, not all people obtained freedom. In China, things were very different. A wave of student demonstrations ended in disaster in Beijing's Tianamen Square when government forces crushed the opposition movement.

Nor was all well in Russia; despite Gorbachev's reforms, the economy was still in crisis, and society seemed to be in a state of collapse. Russia was divided between those who thought there had been too much change and those who felt that there had not been enough. One of the latter was Boris Yeltsin who, in 1991, became the first popularly elected leader of Russia, the largest of the different republics that together made up the USSR.

In August 1991, army hardliners attempted to overthrow Gorbachev. The **coup** was defeated by troops loyal to Gorbachev and he was soon reinstated. Yet, within four months, the Communist Party had been outlawed in the Russian Republic, and the Soviet Union had ceased to exist: all fifteen member republics had declared their independence. Three of the largest states, Russia, the Ukraine and Belorussia, formed a new union called the Commonwealth of Independent States. The last leader of the USSR was now a president without a country, and he resigned on Christmas Day 1991.

Tasks

1. Create a timeline indicating the changes that took place behind the Iron Curtain, 1980–91.

2. Complete the following table:

	Definition
Glasnost	
Perestroika	

3. Create a spider diagram illustrating the Iron Curtain countries that achieved their freedom from communist control along with the date on which they achieved it.

4. Analyse the collapse of communism in the USSR by filling in the following table:

Condition of country	
Attitudes to reform	
1991 coup	
End of communism	
Gorbachev	

KNOWLEDGE TESTS

Knowledge Test I (Pages 126–31)

1 Why did Stalin wish to establish a buffer zone along the USSR's western borders?

2 Where did the Allied leaders meet in February 1945 to discuss the post-war world?

3 Who attended this meeting?

4 List TWO decisions taken at this meeting.

5 Where did the Allied leaders meet in July 1945 to discuss the post-war world?

6 Who attended this meeting?

7 List TWO decisions taken at this meeting.

8 Which leader first used the phrase 'Iron Curtain'?

9 Name TWO East European countries that were behind the 'Iron Curtain'.

10 Which communist leader fell out with Stalin?

11 The threat of a communist takeover in which country resulted in the Truman Doctrine?

12 What position in the US Government did George Marshall hold?

13 What phrase did Stalin use to condemn the Marshall Plan?

14 Name ONE of the organisations set up by Stalin at this time to ensure tighter control over the 'Iron Curtain'.

15 What was the name of the currency the Western Allies wanted to introduce into Germany in 1948?

16 Name TWO results of the Berlin Blockade.

Knowledge Test II (Pages 135–7)

1 Who was the leader of China's communists?
2 What was the name of the movement led by Chiang Kai-shek?
3 To which island did Chiang Kai-shek flee after China was declared a communist country in 1949?
4 Name ONE way in which the USSR demonstrated its approval of what had happened in China.
5 Name ONE way in which the USA demonstrated its disapproval of what had happened in China.
6 Along which parallel was Korea partitioned in 1945?
7 Who was the leader of North Korea?
8 Who was the leader of South Korea?
9 When did North Korea invade South Korea?
10 Why was the USSR not in a position to stop the UN becoming involved in the conflict in Korea?
11 Which US General led the UN force in Korea?
12 Towards which river did the UN force advance after it landed in Korea?
13 How many Chinese troops invaded North Korea?
14 Why did Truman sack MacArthur?
15 Pilots from which country fought the USA in the aerial battles of the Korean War?
16 Which TWO leaders changed in 1953?
17 What was the DMZ?
18 List TWO results of the Korean War.

Knowledge Test III (Pages 138–40)

1 How did workers in East Germany react to Stalin's death?
2 List THREE things that Khrushchev did, 1955–6, that suggested a change of approach by Moscow.
3 Where did protests first erupt in 1956?
4 List TWO ways in which the USSR responded to these protests.
5 Who was appointed leader of Hungary in October 1956?
6 Who replaced this leader after the USSR invaded Hungary?
7 How did the USSR justify its invasion of Hungary?
8 List THREE reasons why the West did nothing to stop events in Hungary.
9 Roughly, how many people had fled to the West via Berlin by 1962?
10 Give TWO reasons why Khrushchev was worried about what was happening in Berlin.
11 How did Khrushchev try to get the West to leave Berlin in 1958?
12 Why did a new wave of people flee East Berlin in 1960?
13 When was the Berlin Wall erected?
14 What action did the West take in response to the permanent division of Berlin?

Knowledge Test IV (Pages 143–9)

1 Name TWO things that Castro did to annoy the USA.
2 What was the name of the failed CIA attempt to overthrow Castro in 1961?
3 Give ONE reason why Khrushchev was keen to have missile bases in Cuba.
4 List TWO of the options that Kennedy had in dealing with the missile crisis.
5 What was the name of the special committee that advised Kennedy during the missile crisis?
6 What secret deal was struck between Kennedy and Khrushchev?
7 Name ONE consequence of the Cuban Missile Crisis.
8 Which European country ruled Vietnam before 1939?
9 What was the name of the nationalist army led by Ho Chi Minh?
10 Along which parallel was Vietnam divided in 1954?
11 Give ONE reason why the South Vietnamese Government was unpopular with its people.
12 What was the name of the resolution passed by the US Congress allowing the US to fight a war in Vietnam?
13 Name ONE of the chemicals used by the US Air Force during Operation Thunder.
14 Give TWO reasons why the US forces found it difficult to defeat the Vietnamese rebels.
15 What was the name of the counteroffensive launched by the Vietnamese rebels in January 1968?
16 Name TWO strategies used by President Nixon to ensure that the USA could remove itself from the Vietnam War.

Knowledge Test V (Pages 150–4)

1 Who did Alexander Dubček replace as leader of Czechoslovakia in January 1968?
2 Name TWO reforms that Dubček introduced to achieve 'socialism with a human face'.
3 What name was given to the period of reform initiated by Dubček?
4 How did Dubček tell the Czech people to react to the Warsaw Pact invasion of their country?
5 Who replaced Dubček as leader of Czechoslovakia?
6 What was the Brezhnev Doctrine?
7 What was *détente*?
8 List TWO reasons for the deterioration in Sino-Soviet relations in the 1960s.
9 Name ONE way in which improved US–Chinese relations could benefit each country.
10 Name TWO ways in which improved US–USSR relations could benefit each country.
11 Name THREE key agreements reached during the period of détente.
12 Give ONE reason why the USSR invaded Afghanistan.
13 Name TWO ways in which the USA reacted to the Soviet invasion of Afghanistan.
14 Give ONE reason why the USSR ended its conflict with Afghanistan.

Knowledge Test VI (Pages 155–8)

1 What nickname did President Reagan give the USSR?
2 What was SDI?
3 Give FOUR reasons why Gorbachev wanted to cut the USSR's defence spending.
4 What was the name of the weapons agreement reached by the USA and USSR in 1987?
5 Name ONE other military change made by Gorbachev at this time.
6 What did Gorbachev and Bush declare in Malta in 1989?
7 In what year was the Warsaw Pact dissolved?
8 What was *perestroika*?
9 What was *glasnost*?
10 In which year did most 'Iron Curtain' countries break free from Soviet control?
11 What was the name of the Romanian dictator who was executed in 1989?
12 What was Solidarity?
13 Where did the 'Velvet Revolution' take place?
14 What happened in Tianamen Square?
15 Where was Boris Yeltsin elected leader of in 1990?
16 Which group tried to overthrow Gorbachev in 1991?
17 On which date did Gorbachev resign as leader of the USSR?

Germany c1918–41

KNOWLEDGE TEST I (PAGE 55)

1 Food shortages increased; the value of currency fell; during 1918 hundreds of thousands of Germans died during a 'flu pandemic.
2 A civilian government would obtain fairer peace terms from the Allies; the new government would get the blame for ending the war.
3 Kiel.
4 9 November 1918.
5 Friedrich Ebert.
6 Armistice agreed.
7 Most ordinary Germans had been led to believe that the war was going well.
8 Spartacists.
9 Rosa Luxemburg and Karl Liebknecht.
10 A right-wing volunteer army made up mainly of former soldiers who detested communism.
11 They were a right-wing group while the government was left wing.
12 Munich.
13 Germany's new constitution was drawn up in Weimar.
14 Usually resulted in weak coalition governments.
15 Allowed the President to rule using emergency decrees in a political crisis when the government could not get enough support from parliament.
16 Meant that the elected government was not running the country, which was undemocratic.
17 France, Belgium or Poland. (Any one)
18 100,000.
19 Germany had to accept all blame for causing the war.
20 It turned them against the government even more.

KNOWLEDGE TEST II (PAGE 56)

1 Wolfgang Kapp.
2 The reduction in the size of the army as demanded by the Treaty of Versailles.
3 The army refused to put down the *putsch*.
4 Sent the Free Corps in to crush their strike.
5 Walter Rathenau.
6 £6,600 million.
7 In December 1922 the Weimar Government announced that it would not be able to meet the next reparation payment.
8 Ordered the population of the Ruhr to engage in passive resistance.
9 The richest part of the country was not producing anything thus reducing the country's income.
   The government had to start importing the goods not being produced, costing more money.
   The workers of the Ruhr still had to be paid even though they were not working.
10 Massive reduction in the value of money.

11 Middle class and poor.
12 He ordered an end to passive resistance to start the economy working again. Government spending was sharply reduced.
He agreed to resume paying reparations, realising that this was the only way to get the French and Belgians out of the Ruhr.
In November 1923 he announced the establishment of a new national bank and the introduction of a new currency, the Rentenmark. (Any three)
13 Allowed Germany to pay a reduced amount of reparations for several years and gave a longer time to pay overall.
14 £1,800 million.
15 Germany, France and Belgium agreed to accept their common borders.
16 League of Nations.

KNOWLEDGE TEST III (PAGE 56)

1 There were no more *putsches*.
Results of the 1928 General Election indicated that people were supporting the moderate parties of the Weimar Republic not the extremist parties such as the Nazis or Communists.
The 1928 election resulted in the establishment of the stable Grand Coalition. (Any one)
2 The anti-democratic Paul von Hindenburg was elected President in 1925.
Parties were getting on better because there was nothing significant for them to fall out over. (Any one)
3 Heavy industry recovered quickly.
Exports rose.
Social welfare provision improved.
Infrastructure was developed. (Any one)
4 Industry was growing unsteadily.
Agriculture was in a depression.
Unemployment was on the increase.
Welfare costs were up.
The government was spending more than it was making.
The loans Germany was receiving from the USA. (Any one)

5 Austria.
6 Worked as a spy for the army.
7 DAP – German Workers' Party.
8 25 Point Programme.
9 The Treaty of Versailles had to be destroyed.
The need for *lebensraum*.
The need for strong government.
A desire to unite all Germans, whilst excluding the Jews. (Any one)
10 The Nazis' private army.
11 November.
12 Ludendorff.
13 The Bavarian government leaders ordered the army to stop the intended *putsch*.
14 By using it to condemn the Weimar Republic and to spread his ideas.
15 Nine months.
16 *Mein Kampf.*
17 Instead of using force to overthrow the Weimar Republic, the Nazis would use the political system.
18 This stressed complete obedience to Hitler.
19 SS and Hitler Youth. (Any one)
20 Won twelve seats.

KNOWLEDGE TEST IV (PAGE 57)

1 Wall Street Crash and death of Stresemann.
2 Prices and wages fell.
Businesses went bankrupt.
Millions lost their jobs.
Banks were closing their doors, resulting in a loss of savings for millions. (Any two)
3 Müller.
4 Collapse of Grand Coalition.
5 Heinrich Brüning
6 107.
7 Hunger Chancellor.
8 Reduced public spending.
Imposed tariffs on imports.
Slashed unemployment benefits.
Introduced wage cuts for civil servants. (Any two)
9 Six million.
10 Hindenburg did not get enough votes in the first election to win.
11 Von Papen.
12 230.
13 Von Papen wanted to gain support for his government.
14 196.
15 Von Schleicher advised the President that the German army would no longer support von Papen governing through the use of Article 48. Von Papen was sacked and von Schleicher appointed.
16 57 days.
17 30 January 1933.

KNOWLEDGE TEST V (PAGE 57)

1 The Reichstag.
The Cabinet.
The President.
The army.
Other parties.
The trade union movement.
State governments. (Any three)
2 Blamed the Communists for it.
3 Decree For the Protection of People and State.
4 288.
5 Stopped opponents attending the vote.
Did a deal with the Centre Party.
Used intimidation in the Reichstag. (Any two)
6 Allowed Hitler to introduce laws without the Reichstag's approval for four years.
7 Co-ordination of all aspects of life to fit in with Nazi ideals.
8 They were banned.
9 July.
10 Abolished all of Germany's state governments apart from Prussia's
11 Ernst Röhm.
12 Röhm wanted a second revolution.
Röhm wanted the SA to become Germany's new army.
13 Hitler feared the army. It was the only group that could challenge his power and authority.
Hitler needed the army. Many of its leaders supported his foreign policy aims. (Any one)
14 Night of the Long Knives.
15 Hindenburg.
16 Swore an oath of personal loyalty to him.

KNOWLEDGE TEST VI (PAGE 58)

1 People's community.
2 Dr Joseph Göbbels.
3 Nuremberg.
4 Most newspapers were brought under control by being bought up by *Eher Verlag*, the Nazi publishers.
   Journalists had to be approved by the Nazis.
   The Editors' Law held editors responsible for the content of their newspapers.
   Newspapers that printed stories the regime disapproved of were shut down.
   Newspaper editors went to a daily Propaganda Ministry briefing to be told what to print.
   All radio stations were brought under Nazi control.
   People were encouraged to buy cheap radios made by the Reich Radio Company.
   Loudspeakers were erected in public places. (Any three)
5 Burned them.
6 *Kinder, Kirche und Kuche* - children, church and cooking.
7 Some women – particularly those married or in the professions – were forced from the workplace.
   Giving every newly married couple a loan of 1000 marks, 25 per cent of which was written off for every child born.
   Women who had large families were awarded the Mother's Cross. They also received additional welfare benefits and were liable for lower rates of tax.
   Contraception and abortion were made more difficult to obtain.
   Divorce to end childless marriages was made easier.
   Unmarried mothers were encouraged to live in homes (*Lebensborn*) where racially pure SS men could impregnate them. (Any two)
8 The numbers of women in jobs actually went up in the later 1930s as the drive for rearmament and autarky took off.
9 Jewish teachers and those regarded as unreliable were dismissed.
   Teachers were encouraged to join the NSLB (National Socialist Teachers' League)
   The curriculum was Nazified to reflect the importance of subjects such as History, Biology, Geography and PE.
   Boys were prepared for life in the military while girls were prepared for their role as mothers.
   The SS established special schools to teach Germany's future leaders. (Any three)
10 Castles of Order – schools for high flyers.
11 Leader of the Hitler Youth.
12 *Pimpfen.*
   Deutsches Jungvolk.
   Hitler Jugend.
   Jung Mädel.
   Bund Deutscher Mädel.
   Glaube und Schönheit. (Any two)
13 Edelweiss Pirates.
   Swing Youth.

KNOWLEDGE TEST VII (PAGE 58)

1 An agreement between the German Government and the Catholic Church.
2 Pope Pius XI.
  Bishop Clemens von Galen. (Any one)
3 Pro-Nazi Lutherans.
4 Ludwig Müller.
5 Anti-Nazi Lutherans.
6 Pastor Martin Niemöller.
7 The Nazi Church.
8 Hatred of the Jewish religion and people.
9 Deprived Jews of many of their political and economic rights.
  Made it illegal for Jews and Aryans to marry or engage in sexual relations outside marriage. (Any one)
10 Olympic Games were being held in Berlin.
11 Night of the Broken Glass – a massive outbreak of anti-Jewish persecution.
12 Criminals.
  The 'work shy'.
  Gypsies.
  Homosexuals.
  The 'anti-social'.
  Jews. (Any two)
13 SS.
14 *Kraft Durch Freude* – Strength Through Joy.
15 The scale of existing public work schemes was increased with the establishment of the National Labour Service (RAD – *Reichsarbeitsdienst*).
  Many people – especially professional women and Jews – were forced from the workplace and their jobs were then given to those who were unemployed. Neither of these groups was then counted as unemployed.
  The introduction of conscription in 1935. As Germany moved to prepare for war, thousands of jobs were created in the armament and associated industries. Likewise the drive for autarky resulted in the creation of new industries focused on creating synthetic replacements for raw materials. (Any two)
16 President of the Reichsbank. Minister of Economics.
17 A plan to ensure that was Germany economically self sufficient during any future conflict (an autarky).
18 Not fully – by 1939 Germany was still importing over 30 per cent of its raw materials.

KNOWLEDGE TEST VIII (PAGE 59)

1 To restore Germany's military strength by removing the military restrictions imposed by the Treaty of Versailles.
  To unite all those claiming German nationality into the Third Reich (*grossdeutschland*).
  To create *lebensraum* (living space) by acquiring new territory in the East to support the growing German population. (Any two)
2 World Disarmament Conference.
  League of Nations. (Any one)
3 Poland.
4 1935.
5 A meeting where the leaders of Britain, France and Italy condemned German infringements of the Treaty of Versailles.
6 Anglo-German Naval Agreement.
7 Rhineland.
8 The prevention of aggression by using negotiation.
9 Rome–Berlin Axis.
  Anti-Comintern Pact. (Any one)
10 The name given to the *Luftwaffe* units that took part in the Spanish Civil War.

11 Hitler told his generals that he envisaged Germany being involved in a major war by the mid 1940s.

12 In 1934 Italy was stronger than Germany and suspicious of her. By 1938 Italy was Germany's main ally and much weaker militarily.

13 Artur Seyss-Inquart.

14 There were three million Germans living there.

15 Czechoslovakia.
USSR.

16 USSR.

17 Invasion of Britain.

18 USSR.

Peace, War and Neutrality: Britain, Northern Ireland and Ireland and the Second World War c1932–49

KNOWLEDGE TEST I (PAGE 88)

1 James MacNeill.

2 *An seanasca.*

3 1933.

4 Abdication crisis.

5 Repayment to Britain of money lent to purchase land in nineteenth century.

6 Between 1922 and 1932 the money had been collected by the Irish Government and passed on to London.

7 Ireland was experiencing the effects of an economic depression.
Northern Ireland had been left off its share on land annuities. (Any one)

8 Twenty per cent.

9 By placing taxes on goods coming from Britain and Northern Ireland.

10 Coal–Cattle Pact.

11 35 per cent reduction in cattle exports. Fall in living standards. (Any one)

12 Peat.

13 1937.

14 *Bunreacht na hÉireann.*

15 The name of the state became Éire. The leader of the government was to be the *Taoiseach.*
A new (largely ceremonial) Head of State would be elected every seven years. That person would be given the title of President. (Any one)

16 Political jurisdiction over the whole island.

17 He believed it would make it easier to end partition.

18 Douglas Hyde.

19 Chose to regard the changes introduced as insignificant.

20 Called a general election.

KNOWLEDGE TEST II (PAGE 89)

1 Neutrality.
  Rearmament.
  Appeasement.
2 People still remembered the horrors of the Great War and were keen that the government did not commit itself to another conflict.
  Britain's economy was still recovering from the impact of the Great War and the Great Depression. Thus it was not in a position to bear the costs of rapid rearmament.
  Many politicians – particularly British Prime Minister Neville Chamberlain – viewed Hitler as a reasonable man with reasonable demands who could be dealt with by reasonable policies.
3 Austria.
  Czechoslovakia.
4 He was confident that the August 1939 Nazi-Soviet Pact neutralised Russia as an opponent.
5 He wanted Éire on his side given the growing tensions in Europe.
6 He wanted to safeguard Éire's neutrality and believed that British control of the Treaty Ports undermined Éire's claims to such neutrality.
7 £10 million.
8 Believed they would be strategically important for Britain if war broke out.
9 Feared the improvement in Anglo-Irish relations might result in an end to partition.
10 As Britain had ignored IRA demands to leave Northern Ireland.
11 Both governments introduced emergency measures.
12 Feared nationalist reaction.
13 £6 million.
14 Short and Harland aircraft factory.
  Harland and Wolff shipyard.

KNOWLEDGE TEST III (PAGE 89)

1 The administration believed that Northern Ireland was beyond the range of enemy aircraft.
2 Nearly two years.
3 German forces had reached the Channel.
4 John MacDermott.
5 The rapid erection of public air-raid shelters.
  The reinforcement of the emergency services.
  Efforts to evacuate children from Belfast. (Any two)
6 April–May 1941.
7 Limited number anti-aircraft guns.
  Insufficient air cover.
  Public shelters capable of housing no more than a quarter of the city's population. (Any two)
8 ARP wardens were not taken seriously.
  Blackouts were routinely ignored.
  The majority of people did not carry gas masks until after the Belfast Blitz. (Any two)
9 Over half a million rifles were ordered from the USA.
  Factories worked multiple shifts to produce aircraft, tanks and heavy weapons.
  The Local Defence Volunteers was established in May 1940.
10 The invasion of Britain.
11 The RAF's control of the skies would prevent a German sea invasion.
12 August 1940.
13 Started to bomb London.
14 As a response to RAF bombing raids on Berlin.
15 Allowed the RAF to regroup and obtain much-needed new aircraft.

KNOWLEDGE TEST IV (PAGE 90)

1 The Germans were aware of the key role that a number of Belfast's industries were playing in the war effort.
Northern Ireland was playing an important strategic role in the war.
2 Close to 1000.
3 Over 56,000.
4 Six months.
5 J M Andrews.
6 Voted against government candidates in two by-elections.
7 Basil Brooke.
8 Ernest Bevin.
9 Feared nationalist reaction.
10 About 83,000.
11 Instead of open enrolment the Northern Ireland Home Guard was based around the B Specials.
The force came under the control of the RUC rather than the army.

12 Naval bases provided services for those vessels involved in the Battle of the Atlantic.
Naval bases acted as bases for vessels keeping sea-lanes open.
Air bases were significantly involved in providing much needed cover to convoys.
Northern Ireland was also used as a base for preparations for D Day. (Any two)
13 Continued availability of fertilisers.
The more than one-hundred-fold increase in tractor numbers.
Basil Brooke. (Any two)
14 Fresh meat, dairy produce and fuel.
15 60,000.
16 Bad management.
Questionable working practices.
A series of strikes. (Any two)

KNOWLEDGE TEST V (PAGE 90)

1 The next day.
2 Supported it.
3 Emergency Powers Act.
4 Army and Local Defence Volunteers increased.
Navy extended.
Air force set up.
5 To invite the British army in to help repel any German invasion.
6 Two.
7 German pilots who bailed out over Ireland were imprisoned while Allied airmen were allowed to cross the border into Northern Ireland.
During the Belfast Blitz, de Valera authorised the dispatch of fire engines to assist.
Allied airmen were permitted to fly over Irish territory through their use of the 'Donegal Air Corridor'.
De Valera allowed the RAF to establish a number of secret radar bases on Irish territory.

8 Six.
9 He visited the German Ambassador to express sympathy over Hitler's death.
10 Dublin was bombed several times.
The Ministry of Supplies was set up under Lemass to ensure that Ireland was not left totally without essential materials.
Ireland benefited from a food surplus.
The lack of available fertilisers damaged the productivity.
Tea, sugar and butter had to be rationed.
Fruit and chocolate became unavailable.
Smuggling increased.
The closure of factories had an impact on employment levels and many Irish people began to seek their fortunes in Britain.
The harsh economic situation meant that Fianna Fáil still lost ten seats in the 1943 general election. (Any six)

KNOWLEDGE TEST VI (PAGE 91)

1 Clement Attlee.
2 Britain was close to bankruptcy.
   Poverty was widespread.
   Most manufactured goods were being exported to pay for food imports.
   There were acute shortages of coal, whilst bread and potatoes had to be rationed for the first time in 1946. (Any two)
3 Bringing private companies/industries under government control.
4 Feared the impact on their independence.
   Feared the impact on their income.
5 Fear of the cost.
   Fear that it would increase London's influence over Northern Ireland.
6 To demonstrate its gratitude for Northern Ireland's contribution to the war effort.
7 Northern Ireland Housing Trust.
8 Guaranteed all children over 11 free secondary education up to the age of 15 for the first time. Gave those who passed the 11+ examination the opportunity to attend grammar schools.
9 Unemployment shot up.
   Building materials became almost unobtainable. As a result new homes could not be built.
   Coal imports withheld by Britain.
   Éire experienced a harsh winter and severe fuel shortages in 1947.
   Rationing remained in force and was extended to include bread from the start of 1947.
   Emigration rates remained high. (Any two)
10 Fine Gael.
   Two different Labour parties.
   Clann na Talmhan.
   Clann na Poblachta. (Any two)
11 Set up the Industrial Development Authority (IDA).
   Started a programme to build new houses.
   Signed a trade agreement with Britain in 1948. (Any one)
12 Easter Monday 1949.
13 The right to sit in the Dáil.
14 Chapel Gate Election.
15 'In no event will Northern Ireland…cease to be part of…the United Kingdom without the consent of the parliament of Northern Ireland'.

Changing Relationships: Britain, Northern Ireland and Ireland c1965–85

KNOWLEDGE TEST I (PAGE 123)

1 Lord Brookeborough.
2 O'Neill's leadership was weakened by the fact that most of the Unionist Party's MPs had wanted Brian Faulkner as Prime Minister.
3 £900 million of investment to update existing industries and attract new ones.
   Transport infrastructure modernised (road and rail).
   Co-operation with the Dublin-based Irish Trades Union Congress (ITUC), whose support was important for economic development.
   Economic Council established under Brian Faulkner.
   Ministry of Development set up to drive economic revival.
   The establishment of a new city called Craigavon.
   The development of a new university in Coleraine. (Any three)

4   A number of multinational firms (Michelin, DuPont, Goodyear, ICI, Grundig) opened factories in Northern Ireland.
A motorway system was begun.
An oil refinery was opened in Belfast.
A new airport was under development.
An agreement regarding the supply of electricity was agreed with Dublin. (Any two)

5   In total over 35,000 new jobs were created during the 1960s, but at the same time over 20,000 were lost in the ailing traditional industries such as linen manufacture.
Between 1963 and 1969 money had to be given to shipbuilders Harland and Wolff to keep it afloat.
Unemployment averaged between 7 and 8 per cent.
Several companies refused government grants to open factories west of the Bann, seeing the area as too remote from their export markets. (Any two)

6   Meeting with Lemass and Lynch.
Visiting Cardinal William Conway, spiritual leader of Ireland's Catholics.
Offering official condolences on the death of Pope John XXIII.

Visiting schools and hospitals run by the Catholic Church.
Increasing the financial support provided for Catholic hospitals and schools. (Any three)

7   Rev Ian Paisley.

8   Influence of Catholic Church.
Articles II and III of the Republic's constitution.

9   Brian Faulkner.
Harry West.

10 The Nationalist Party took up the role of official opposition in Stormont for the first time in its history.

11 Most economic development was in Protestant areas.
Unemployment was at a higher level west of the Bann.
Despite significant cross-community protest, the new university was sited in the mainly Protestant town of Coleraine, rather than in the mainly nationalist Derry/Londonderry, Northern Ireland's second city.
No significant attempts were made to increase Catholic membership of various health and education bodies. (Any two)

KNOWLEDGE TEST II (PAGE 123)

1   The US Civil Rights Movement and the student demonstrations that had taken place in France in the same year.

2   Achieve one man, one vote.
Ensure the fair allocation of council houses.
End gerrymandering.
Prevent discrimination in the allocation of government jobs.
Remove the operation of the Special Powers Act.
Disband the B Specials.
Establish a formal complaints procedure against local authorities to report breaches in the above areas. (Any three)

3   A new generation of Catholics.
Some Protestants.
Communists.
Academics.
Trade unionists. (Any two)

4   NICRA was seen as provocative.
Some felt that the movement was nothing more than a front for the IRA.
Others believed that it was only interested in Catholic rights and would undermine the position of Protestants.
Some thought that that the movement was a threat to the continued existence of Northern Ireland. (Any two)

5   Coalisland to Dungannon.

6 The march was met by violence from the police.
7 NICRA going ahead with marches that had been banned by the government. Marches were seen as provocative, especially when they went through Protestant areas.
   NICRA marches coming into contact with Unionist counter-demonstrations. (Any one)
8 The allocation of council housing on a points system.
   The replacement of Londonderry Corporation by a Development Commission.
   The removal of parts of the Special Powers Act.
   Reforms within local government,

including the ending of extra votes for business owners.
   The appointment of an ombudsman to investigate complaints. (Any two)
9 To appeal for calm.
10 People's Democracy.
11 Burntollet Bridge.
12 An official investigation into Northern Ireland's increasing violence.
13 Brian Faulkner.
14 There was a reduction in unionist support and divisions of loyalty among the unionist MPs elected.
   There was little or no evidence of support from Catholic voters.
   O'Neill nearly lost his own seat to Ian Paisley. (Any one)
15 Major James Chichester Clark.

KNOWLEDGE TEST III (PAGE 124)

1 A violent conflict between nationalists and police in Derry/Londonderry in August 1969.
2 A statement of reassurance for nationalists and unionists.
3 One man, one vote and an end to gerrymandering.
   A committee on policing was established under Lord Hunt.
   The Scarman Tribunal was set up to investigate recent disturbances.
   A single housing authority was established, taking over housing functions from local councils.
   Measures to prevent discrimination in public employment.
   A £2 million programme of work-creating schemes
   Increases in investment grants. (Any four)
4 It recommended disarming the RUC and disbanding the B Specials.
5 Official IRA.
   Provisional IRA.
6 Civil rights.
   Defence of the Catholic population.

The destruction of the Stormont Government.
   The removal of 'British imperialism' from Ireland. (Any two)
7 As a source of protection.
8 In July 1970 the army imposed a 34-hour curfew on the Lower Falls area while houses were searched for weapons. This damaged the army's relationship with the nationalist community and helped increase IRA membership.
9 UDA.
10 Brian Faulkner.
11 Democratic Unionist Party (DUP).
   Alliance Party (APNI).
   Social Democratic and Labour Party (SDLP). (Any two)
12 Internment.
13 A riot developed and in response troops from the Parachute Regiment shot 13 men dead; 13 more were injured, one of whom subsequently died of his wounds.
14 Lord Widgery.
15 Vanguard.

KNOWLEDGE TEST IV (PAGE 124)

1 By suspending Stormont and introducing Direct Rule.
2 William Whitelaw.
3 Bloody Friday.
   Claudy bomb.
4 A British army operation to regain control of the paramilitary-controlled no-go areas.
5 A role for the Republic of Ireland in the running of Northern Ireland.
6 A body set up to co-ordinate unionist opposition to power-sharing.
7 The results of the elections to the power-sharing assembly revealed that the number of anti power-sharing unionists elected was greater than the number of unionists elected who supported power-sharing.
8 Brian Faulkner.
   Gerry Fitt.

9 To work out the details of the 'Irish Dimension'.
10 Council of Ireland.
11 1 January 1974.
12 A meeting of the Official Unionist Party's ruling body, the Ulster Unionist Council, on 4 January voted to reject the Sunningdale Agreement.
13 Eleven of the twelve Northern Ireland constituencies were won by anti-Sunningdale candidates.
14 A group of Protestant trade unionists that had gained substantial amounts political and paramilitary support – the Ulster Workers' Council.
15 Dublin.
    Monaghan.
16 Spongers.
17 The army was ordered in to take over fuel supplies.

KNOWLEDGE TEST V (PAGE 125)

1 Constitutional Convention.
2 Reducing the strength of the army in Northern Ireland while increasing the size of the RUC and UDR.
3 Those convicted after March 1976 would be treated in the same way as other criminals.
4 Mairéad Corrigan.
   Betty Williams.
5 Blanket protest.
   Dirty protest.
6 The prisoners believed that a deal had been made.
7 Fermanagh-South Tyrone.
8 Sinn Féin's strategy of contesting elections while also continuing to use extra-constitutional methods to achieve its aims.
9 An assembly, which would be given decision-making powers only if there was cross-community support for power-sharing.

10 Gerry Adams.
11 A united Ireland.
    A federal arrangement.
    Joint authority. (Any two)
12 15 November 1985.
13 FitzGerald hoped that reduced nationalist alienation from the state and reform of the security forces in Northern Ireland would undermine the minority's toleration of the IRA and support for Sinn Féin.
14 Britain accepting that the Republic had a role to play in the government of the North.
    The Republic accepting that a united Ireland was a long-term goal that would only happen with the agreement of a majority of the province's population.
15 Marches to the headquarters of the new Anglo-Irish Secretariat.
    A huge protest rally at Belfast's City Hall on 23 November 1985.

All fifteen unionist MPs resigned their seats at Westminster but then stood for them again in the resulting by-elections. A unionist 'Day of Action' on 3 March 1986.
The launching of a campaign of civil disobedience.

Loyalist paramilitaries engaged in a campaign of violence and intimidation against the RUC.
In November 1986, Ulster Resistance, a paramilitary organisation whose aim was the destruction of the Agreement, was formed. (Any two)

The Cold War c1945–91

KNOWLEDGE TEST I (PAGE 159)

1 To ensure that the USSR would not be invaded again.
2 Yalta.
3 Churchill.
  Roosevelt.
  Stalin.
4 Germany and Berlin would be divided into four zones to be occupied by the Allies and France.
  Germany would pay reparations.
  The United Nations would be established.
  The USSR would declare war on Japan three months after Germany's surrender.
  Agreement over new borders for post-war Poland.
  An agreement that Eastern Europe would come under Soviet influence. (Any two)
5 Potsdam.
6 Churchill (then Attlee).
  Stalin.
  Truman.
7 How Germany was to be divided and occupied.
  How Austria was to be divided and occupied.
  The reparations that each power could take from their own zone. (Any two)
8 Churchill.
9 Albania.
  Bulgaria.
  Hungary.
  Poland.
  Romania.
  USSR. (Any two)
10 Tito.
11 Greece.
12 Secretary of State.
13 'Dollar Diplomacy'.
14 Cominform.
   Comecon. (Any one)
15 Deutschmark.
16 NATO established.
   Warsaw Pact established.
   Germany divided. (Any two)

KNOWLEDGE TEST II (PAGE 160)

1 Mao Zedong.
2 Nationalist Kuomintang (KMT).
3 Formosa (Taiwan).
4 A Treaty of Friendship was agreed between the two powers.
5 Refused to recognise the new regime as China's legitimate government.
   Tried its best to ignore communist China and continued to support Chiang Kai-shek's right to represent China in the UN. (Any one)
6 38th.
7 Kim Il Sung.
8 Syngman Rhee.
9 25 June 1950.
10 The USSR was boycotting the UN.
11 Douglas MacArthur.
12 Yalu.
13 Over 250,000.
14 Because MacArthur disagreed with Truman's decision not to invade China or use nuclear weapons against China.

15 USSR.
16 Stalin.
   Truman.
17 The demilitarised area between North and South Korea.
18 Over two million died in the war.
   Containment worked.
   The relationship between North and South Korea was tense and bitter.
   US–Chinese relations became even tenser.
   America signed a peace treaty with Japan, ended military occupation and invested heavily in the Japanese economy.
   The USA signed agreements with the Philippines, Australia and New Zealand, which confirmed its position as the protector of the region.
   NATO was turned into a full-blown military alliance. (Any two)

KNOWLEDGE TEST III (PAGE 160)

1 Rioted.
2 In 1955 Khrushchev visited Yugoslavia and apologised for the way in which Stalin had treated the country.
   In 1955 Khrushchev agreed to meet the leaders of the West in Geneva; the first such meeting for over a decade.
   In February 1956 Khrushchev delivered an historic speech (known as the Secret Speech) at the Communist Party's twentieth party congress. Khrushchev denounced the policies that Stalin had followed and urged the development of 'peaceful co-existence' with non-communist nations.
   Khrushchev began a policy of destalinisation, aimed at ending the influence of the dead leader over the USSR. (Any three)
3 Poland.

4 Soviet tanks crushed the opposition. Khrushchev also agreed to the appointment of a moderate communist, Wladyslaw Gromulka, as leader and to the introduction of a number of reforms.
5 Imre Nagy.
6 Janos Kadar.
7 Fear of Hungary leaving the Warsaw Pact.
8 The Western powers were preoccupied and divided by the Suez Crisis.
   The USA was in the middle of a presidential election campaign.
   The West felt that it would be much more risky to confront Russia in Eastern Europe than it was to confront communism in Asia.
9 Over two million.
10 It meant a significant loss of manpower.

It implied that people preferred to live under capitalism rather than under communism.

Khrushchev was concerned about West Berlin being used as a 'listening post', enabling the West to gain information about activities behind the Iron Curtain. (Any two)

KNOWLEDGE TEST IV (PAGE 161)

1. He began to nationalise industries and banks, many of which were owned by American businesses.
   In 1960 the USSR and Cuba agreed to trade oil and sugar for machinery.
   In 1961 Castro announced that he had become a communist. (Any two)
2. Bay of Pigs disaster.
3. Missiles in Cuba would be able to reach most US cities.
   Provide a counterbalance to the US missiles that had been installed in countries such as Turkey. (Any one)
4. Do nothing.
   Attack the bases by air.
   Invade Cuba.
   Blockade Cuba. (Any two)
5. ExComm.
6. Kennedy had secretly agreed to remove US missiles in Turkey.
7. A telephone hotline between Washington and Moscow was set up.
   Both sides agreed to begin talks to reduce the number of nuclear weapons on each side. (Any one)
8. France.
9. Vietminh.
10. 17th.
11. The regime was brutal and corrupt.
    The government was made up of mostly Catholic landowners and was out of touch with its people, the majority of whom were Buddhist peasants. (Any one)
12. Tonkin Resolution.
13. Napalm.
    Agent Orange. (Any one)
14. The Vietnamese had already seen off two foreign armies.
    The US army was made up of many inexperienced soldiers (conscripts).
    The USA was fighting an enemy that used guerrilla tactics, dressed in the same way as the Vietnamese peasantry and knew the country well.
    The Vietcong developed a vast network of underground tunnels to support their guerrilla campaign.
    The Vietnamese people had no reason to support the US forces. US tactics, such as gathering peasants into large villages (Strategic Hamlets), annoyed many, while the army seemed prepared to harass and kill civilians in their efforts to root out the Vietcong. (Any two)
15. Tet.
16. Increased the levels of bombing against North Vietnam.
    Ordered secret bombing raids against the neighbouring countries of Cambodia and Laos in 1970.
    Introduced the policy of Vietnamisation. (Any two)

11. He threatened to give East Germany control of access points to the city if the Western powers did not leave.
12. As a result of increased tensions following the U2 incident.
13. August 1961.
14. None.

KNOWLEDGE TEST V (PAGE 161)

1 Antonin Novotny.
2 Freedom of speech and of the press.
   Less centralised economic control.
   Development of foreign trade.
   Removal of restrictions on travel abroad.
   Reduction in powers of secret police.
   (Any two)
3 Prague spring.
4 Passive resistance.
5 Gustav Husak.
6 Brezhnev's justification for the invasion of Czechoslovakia. It stated that it was the duty of communist countries to act together to prevent another communist state from turning to capitalism.
7 A period of improvement in relations between East and West.
8 Differences over methods of agricultural development.
   China believed Russia wanted to dominate her.
   Russia refused to share nuclear technology.
   China was against Khrushchev's public criticism of Stalin.
   China believed peaceful co-existence was a betrayal of the ideas of Marx and Lenin. It thought Khrushchev was being too soft with the West.
   China condemned the Soviet climbdown over Cuba.
   In 1969 a border dispute between the two powers resulted in the deaths of a number of military personnel. (Any two)
9 Economic benefits such as the opening of new markets to both countries and, in China's case, the possibility of the investment of capital and technological knowledge.
   Military benefits, in that the USA wanted China to put pressure on North Vietnam to negotiate an end to the Vietnam War.
   Diplomatic benefits that meant each country could use the other in their ongoing power struggles with the USSR. (Any one)
10 New understandings that might avoid coming close to nuclear war again.
   The need to cut back on military spending due to the fact that both were facing severe economic problems.
   America needed new export markets and Russia needed foreign supplies of grain. (Any two)
11 SALT I.
   Helsinki Agreement.
   SALT II.
12 Moscow wanted to restore a government friendly to the USSR.
   Russian feared that if the Muslim rebels in Afghanistan succeeded in seizing control it might encourage Muslims living in the Asian areas of the USSR to try to gain freedom from Soviet control. (Any one)
13 Imposed sanctions by stopping US grain exports to Russia.
   The US Congress refused to approve the SALT II Agreement.
   Carter authorised an increase in arms spending.
   The USA also organised a boycott of the 1980 Moscow Olympic Games. (Any two)
14 Russian forces were unable to defeat the rebels.
   The war had become unpopular at home.
   The war was damaging Russia's economy. (Any one)

KNOWLEDGE TEST VI (PAGE 162)

1 The 'evil empire'.
2 Strategic Defence Initiative. A laser defence system that would effectively create a shield around the USA, which could not be penetrated by Russian missiles.
3 Living standards were appallingly low. There were significant levels of corruption within the Communist Party. Millions were on the verge of starvation because of the poor performance of the agricultural sector.
   Much of Russia's industry was in dire need of modernisation.
   Technologically, Russia was decades behind the West.
   The war in Afghanistan was draining billions from the economy. (Any four)
4 INF (Intermediate Nuclear Forces) Treaty.
5 The withdrawal of Soviet forces from Afghanistan.
   A huge reduction in the size of the Soviet armed forces.
   The withdrawal of troops from other Iron Curtain countries. (Any one)
6 That the Cold War was over.
7 1991.
8 Restructuring of the Russian economy through the introduction of more western-style policies.
9 Openness – freedom to debate, freedom for the media, freedom from government control.
10 1989.
11 Nicolae Ceausescu.
12 A Polish trade union. The first free trade union set up behind the Iron Curtain.
13 Czechoslovakia.
14 A wave of student demonstrations ended in disaster in Beijing's Tianamen Square when government forces crushed the opposition movement.
15 Russia.
16 Army hardliners.
17 25 December 1991.

GLOSSARY

Abdicate To give up the position of king or queen of a country.

Abdication crisis The time in 1936 when Britain's King Edward VIII abdicated so that he could marry a divorced American woman, Wallis Simpson.

Allies The name given Britain, France, the USA and Russia during the World Wars I and II.

Anschluss Union between Austria and Germany.

Anti-Semitism Anti-Jewish ideas.

Appeasement The policy of making concessions to an opponent in the hope that they will stop making demands.

Apprentice Boys A loyalist club set up to remember the group of apprentices who closed the gates of Derry/Londonderry against the armies of King James II in 1689.

Ard Fheis Annual Party Conference (Irish).

Armistice A truce or ceasefire.

Autarky Economic self-sufficiency – not having to rely on other countries for supplies.

Backbencher An MP who is a member of the government party but who does not have a job in the government.

Barter economy When goods rather than money are given in exchange for some service or other.

Blitzkrieg Rapid land and air attack (lightning war).

Boycott To cut off connections with a person, group or organisation.

Capitalist An economic system (or a person supporting it) that believes in private ownership and the making of profits.

Censorship Prevention of the publication of unwanted viewpoints.

CIA Central Intelligence Agency. A US government body set up in 1947 to collect information on foreign groups and governments.

Civil disobedience Protesting peacefully against alleged injustice.

Civil service A government's administrative support.

Civil war A war between members of the same nation.

Coalition A government made up of different political parties.

Communism The ideas of Karl Marx who supported a system of rule where industries were run by the government for the good of the people.

Concordat Agreement between a state and the Catholic Church.

Congress The US parliament.

Conscription/Conscripts Compulsory military service and those that serve.

Constitution A document setting out the rules by which a country is to be run.

Constitutional monarchy A system where power is shared between a monarch and a parliament.

Containment A policy introduced by the USA to stop the spread of communism.

Coup Usually a violent overthrow of a government by a military force.

Demilitarise Ensure area does not have a military presence.

Democracy System whereby the people freely elect a government on a regular basis

Destalinisation A policy introduced by Khrushchev that aimed at removing the influence of Stalin over the USSR.

Détente The easing of hostility or strained relations between countries.

Devolved/Devolution A political system

where local parliaments are given some powers by the central parliament.

Diktat *A dictated peace (German).*

Direct Rule The system by which Northern Ireland was ruled directly from Westminster and not by its own local parliament.

Discrimination Acting in an unfair way towards people of a different race or religion.

Dominion A self-governing colony.

Domino theory The fear that once one country fell to communism, neighbouring countries would do likewise.

Fascist/Fascism A set of political ideas developed by Benito Mussolini in Italy. Based on extreme nationalist ideas.

Federal A political system with a central and local parliaments each with their own areas of responsibility.

Führerprinzip *Complete obedience to the leader.*

General election An election held for all the seats in a parliament.

Gerrymandering The practice of drawing electoral boundaries in a way that benefits one particular group at the expense of another.

Gleichschaltung *Co-ordination of all aspects of life to fit in with Nazi ideals.*

Governor General Representative of the monarch in a dominion.

Guerrilla *A war where one side tends to use hit and run tactics against a superior enemy.*

Hyperinflation Massive increases in prices.

Imperialism The idea of a country having colonies.

Indoctrinate To try and force people to believe in a certain set of ideas.

Interned/ Internment Imprisonment without trial.

Irish Dimension The idea that the Irish Government should have some input into how Northern Ireland is governed.

Iron Curtain A phrase used by Winston Churchill to explain how Europe had been divided between capitalism and communism.

Judiciary The system of judges and courts.

Kaiser Emperor of Germany (1871–1918)

League of Nations A body established by the Paris Peace Settlement in 1919 in an attempt to provide a place where leaders could talk together and so avoid wars.

Lebensraum *Living space.*

Luftwaffe *German Air Force.*

Marxism The ideas of Karl Marx. (See communism.)

Moderator The leader of a church (usually Presbyterian).

Mujaheddin Muslim rebels who operate in Afghanistan.

Muslim A follower of the teachings of the Prophet Mohammed (known as Islam).

National Security Council A group that advises the US President on foreign policy issues.

Nationalise/Nationalisation To bring under the ownership/control of the nation.

Nationalist A person who seeks to protect the interests of a particular nation.

Nazism The ideology of National Socialist German Workers' Party. Based on extreme nationalist ideas.

Official opposition The second largest party in a parliament.

Ombudsman An official who deals with complaints from the public.

Paris Peace Settlement The name given to a number of treaties drawn up at the end of the First World War.

Partition/ Partitioning The artificial division of a country.

Passive resistance To oppose a group without using violence.

Plebiscite A type of referendum. A special vote where all the people of a country decide on a particular issue.

Privy Council Part of the British judicial system.

Propaganda Political advertising.

Proportional representation A system of voting designed to create a result more in line with the way in which people voted.

'Puppet' government A government under the control of another power.

Radar A system of using radio pulses to detect the location of aircraft and other objects.

Rates A payment made by householders to their local council.

Reparations The fine placed on Germany at the end of World War I.

Republic A form of government with no monarch.

Republican Believer in a republic.

Sanctions A penalty imposed (usually on an organisation or nation) for not doing something.

Secretariat A group of civil servants supporting the work of the Anglo-Irish Agreement.

Secretary of State A politician who is in charge of a government department and who is usually a member of the Cabinet. In the USA the term refers specifically to the Foreign Minister.

Sectarian To think or act in a way that discriminates against those of another religious group.

Special category status The recognition that those convicted of crimes connected with the 'Troubles' had acted for political and not criminal reasons.

Stormont The name given to the Northern Ireland Parliament building opened in 1932.

Summit A meeting between leaders of different countries.

Taoiseach The prime minister of the Republic of Ireland.

TD Member of *Dáil Éireann* (*Teachta Dála* – deputy to the Dáil).

The 'Troubles' The name given to the period of violence in Northern Ireland that began in the late 1960s.

Tribunal A body set up to reach a decision on a particular issue.

Unionist A person who wishes the political union between Great Britain and Northern Ireland to continue.

UUUC United Ulster Unionist Council – an anti-power-sharing umbrella grouping comprising the Official Unionists, the DUP and the Vanguard Unionist Progressive Party, set up by William Craig to oppose power-sharing.

UVF Ulster Volunteer Force. A paramilitary group originally set up in 1912 to oppose the introduction of Home Rule to Ireland.

Veto The right to prevent or forbid an action or decision taking place.

Vietnamisation President Nixon's policy of reducing US involvement in Vietnam by getting locals to do the fighting.

Volksgemeinschaft People's community.

Welfare State A system where the government provides educational and health facilities for the people of a nation.